Humans Cursed by Geography on the Pursuit of Happiness

My two –three–Memoirs in one Manuscript

True to Fact Stories

Cristina G.

To Valentina, my siblings and all people who were forced to emigrate in the search of a better life

Acknowledgements

A colossal Thank You to Dane Newman who proofread and corrected (for free) the first part of this book. The second part was proofread professionally.

A big Thank You to those who took the trouble to let me know about a few inconsistencies in the text.

Martin, Martine, Simone, Monica, Laura, Valentina your constant support is priceless. I can't thank you enough.

Valentina, thank you for the oranges, I enjoyed them very much.

A massive Thank You to the reviewers who ignored my poor English language (as I insisted) and stood by my side in this long learning process. I am getting better day by day.

Thank you to everyone who shares and appreciates my work.

Thank you all for your understanding and care. It's touching.

May the universe be always on your side.

Prologue

Because some of my readers have asked me, here are both (including the Missing Chapter from Asiago/Italy) of my memoirs in one manuscript.

.

Oranges at Christmas in a Communist Country

Preface

This is a fragment of my communist childhood—true to fact—and I have spent more than a year to build the courage to publish it.

I didn't write it for sympathy, but because it's a great story and deserves some notability. I believe that many of us could write at least one book about their lives.

As you'll soon realise, my English is a work in progress. Nevertheless, I would like to ask you to focus on the story and not on my grammar or spelling. I know it could be hard at times, but I did what I could to the best of my present abilities.

People whom I asked advice and feedback told me that I should wait until my English is ready to be shown in books. I couldn't agree more. However, I am not twenty anymore, and cannot postpone this forever. I am a forty-one-perfectionist woman, and it could take me fifteen years, or the rest of my life, to feel satisfied with my English skills. It is now or never.

I beg you to be tolerant and to give me a chance as most of my stories are simply extraordinary. Publishing this first short fragment of my life means everything to me, and you'll soon find out why.

I thank you from the bottom of my heart for your trust and understanding. I hope you won't find it too difficult to read. I know some people didn't.

***

The double marks ("") are for quoting and direct speech. The single marks (') are for mind's thoughts.

What is Communism?

How old were you when you've discovered that Santa Claus was not a real person?

I was nine.

I am sure you have heard many stories about Communism. Some terrible, others not that much. While I was living in Italy and in England, I met people born in various communist countries. They all have different stories to tell the world. Mine was a thousand miles away.

Every communist country has its own system. Some governments are stricter than others. Some Rulers give less and pretend more from their people. But I didn't know anything about this until a few years back. I always thought that Communism was the same in every country on Earth.

It seemed that Romania was alone in Europe. It didn't respond to USSR or any other Political Power. Gorbachev visited my country often but Ceausescu wasn't very fond of him. I don't know much on the subject, so I'll stop here.

What I know is that I am the tenth child of a family of eleven. It was God's decision for me to come into this world, more of an incident if you want. Most definitely not a desired or planned child. Like my siblings and almost all children of that epoch though. My mother was forty when she gave birth to me in the middle of November 1975. She didn't have any real employment, as we intend it, but wasn't a housewife either, my mother was a slave on her own land.

Now, if you lived in my communist country and were a farmer, you know what I mean, but if you didn't, the word *slave* will sound extreme and make you feel I am overemphasising, except I am not.

The Communism period in my country started in 1948 with the king—Michael I— forced to abdicate and ended in blood in December 1989.

Communism, on paper, is an outstanding theory, "A system of social organisation in which all property is owned by the community, each person contributes and receives according to their ability and needs." — says Wikipedia. A Utopia I would say, and how many of these Utopias do you know of in this world?

Let me tell you in my words what Communism represented for my family. Please forgive my ignorance in politics, it is not something I would invest my time in.

Before Communism, my parents' families own several hectares of land, among other properties. They were considered wealthy farmers. They worked their land, raised animals and everything they had belonged to them. Others had goods, many were much wealthier than others, and some were even more: the boyars. There was a clear separation of social classes, but from what my parents told me, these rich people, boyars, were very good human beings and gave work to the poor.

My mother as a child, before her parents became wealthy, used to work for one of these boyars. He was a kind person and was used to give many presents to children on their birthdays, for example. He would come with bags full of candies, fruits, and various other things offering them to the celebrated of the day. They were not required to do that, it was a personal choice.

Now, I am sure you think that he was horrible regardless of these gifts because he employed children to work on his properties and that was inhuman. I couldn't agree more. I am telling you, it's how I always thought and sustained; however, we forget one fundamental thing here, back then, seventy years ago, more and less, that was considered absolutely normal. There were no laws that stated it was illegal to hire children and make them work for several hours a day. Things have changed a lot since then, although you'll still find adults exploiting children and not only in my country. We all know that. It is not my place to speak about this though.

When the Communism was imposed in the country, farmers and boyars with no exceptions were forced to put all their land together to form a collective.

When I say forced, it means that soldiers came with guns and tanks and pointed them directly at innocent people. Whoever refused the *new commandments* were killed on sight or cast into prisons, where they were badly tortured and left to starve to death on the cement floors of their cells. Many people died, hundreds, instantly shot dead.

All boyars were taken from their houses and sent to sleep in the middle of the street. After a life of hard work, everything they earned was confiscated by the state.

The farmers, after being deprived of their land, would still be owners on paper, and work the land, except that it wasn't for themselves, but for the greater good, the country.

You won't read about these atrocities in history

books because Communism is still a utopia for many.

I wasn't born yet, and I considered myself lucky to have not witnessed any of that. But my parents were, and you won't believe it, but they never said a word about this until the Communism had dissipated.

Why? Fear. Stories of entire families massacred circulated among people. My parents would have never risked our lives. They accepted the new lifestyle and imposed themselves to forget the past.

Husband and wife didn't speak a word between them, parents and children were afraid one of another. "Shh, even the walls have ears," my dad used to say. I came to learn all these things from my parents and other elderly people I got to talk to after the Communism—there weren't many left.

After the deprivation of goods and land, luckily, following certain criteria most were allowed to keep a piece of land attached to their houses for surviving purposes. Farmers lived off of the production from that soil. As I was saying, my mother and us, all farmers really, infant or elderly, were slaves on our land.

From March to late November six days a week, sometimes seven, my mother would wake up at four or five in the morning to cook for the family, then she'd go to various locations to do her part for the greater good. Twelve to fifteen hours each day, no matter the weather, physical conditions, or personal issues. There were no excuses, except for when the earth was oversaturated with water, from too much rain, and no being, human or animal, could walk on it.

My brothers and sisters, myself included, would go to school, mostly in the mornings, then would come home, get changed out of our uniforms into farmers' attire and reach my mother in the fields. Sometimes we would go to a different field that needed to be finished at the same time with the one my mother was working on. It all depended on the state, necessity, and requirement. One of us had to remain home to feed the animals, take care of the house, and cook dinner for everybody.

1975 has been a particularly busy and difficult year for the farmers in the country, especially for those from my region. It rained a lot, and all the harvests have been delayed by weeks or months. Winter had come, and the fields were covered in snow. It didn't matter though, the beetroots and the corn had to be cropped and the land prepared for the next year production.

Every new scholastic year started with two, three or even more weeks of hand-work on the fields. It wasn't an option, it was compulsory. The schools were asked to help because the adults weren't able to do all the work by themselves. Each family had a determined amount of production to deliver or a precise number of hectares to work on during each year. About how much was decided by the people in charge based on several criteria, one was the number of people in a family, parents, and progenies. The more children you had, the more you were required to produce and deliver. That decision was taken on the day one was born.

So you see, the day I came into this world, my family got additional land to work on, and I wasn't able to help out yet. I lived with this burden for years, since I was just a toddler.

Everybody thinks babies cannot interpret what is going on around them, but I don't how I was able to understand even before my birth when I was just a foetus in my mother's womb. I felt my mother's pain and struggle. I cried with her every time she felt blue. And she wasn't a happy soul. I don't remember, of course, but why else would I have been so sensitive, sensible, and responsible from such an early age?

***

You know by now that this story took place in a remote communist country situated in the East of Europe. There weren't many hospitals or doctors in that period of time, but there were a lot of midwives. That was because children in the communist era were considered a gold mine for the country. All women were encouraged and praised to remain pregnant as often as possible.

From 1960 to 1970 the number of births doubled in my country. In 1966 abortion was declared illegal. All this because the Communist Party (PCR) decided that the Romanian population should be increased from 23 to 30 million inhabitants. Just like that.

Women who had more than nine children were rewarded with a sum of money and with various certificates which made them feel valued. 1967 was the year in which the nation's population increased by 100%.

The story of my name

My mother worked the land for all the time she'd carried me, up until the morning I decided I wanted out. The night before, she went to her team leader and asked if she could stay home the next day because something made my mother think my birth due has come. She was afraid I will be born on some fields very far away from the village and getting back on time could have been impossible. But the team leader firmly denied. "Don't be ridiculous, Maria, if that comes, we will find a camion to take you to the maternity house. We can't let anyone home under any circumstances."

It wasn't an excuse; my mother knew her body well. I was the tenth child, of course she felt me kicking and preparing to get out any minute.

The worst part was that her team leader was a woman and a friend.

Great feminism support and demonstration of humanity, right? That was Communism itself, some paid a higher price than others.

It was 3 o'clock on a Friday morning when my mother woke up in terrible pain and realised that I had indeed decided to leave the safety of her belly for a place I knew nothing about.

The whole family was asleep, nine, no wait, eight children and my father. Two of my older sisters were already married and left the family by then.

My mother didn't say a word to anyone, as quiet as

possible washed her face with cold water, put a few clean clothes into a plastic bag as quick as possible, and walked towards the maternity clinic from our village. Luckily, she didn't have to go far, just for five hundred metres. But every woman who gave birth would testify that when your water had broken, you cannot make any step without risking to let your child fall on the ground.

My mother has told me that she'd walked extremely slow, more crawling really and was utterly exhausted when getting there.

I cannot even begin to imagine the pain she must have been through. But the day I asked her how did she cope with it all, pregnancy, pain, birth. My mother said she was used to it and it wasn't such a big deal. That's why she didn't even think to ask someone to accompany her to the maternity house. It was her duty as a mother, nobody else's.

"What about someone to support you or carry your bag, what about dad? I was born from you, but he put me there," I said in shock.

"What do you think he could have done? Help me? How? I was the one who had to push. The only person it was needed to give birth to you it was me, and I was there. Ready to do my duty. Besides, the children had school, and your father had to go to work. There was no way that any of them would have been excused from doing what was required of them. They had their things to do, I had mine. All worked out well, isn't it? You see, there is no need for a second person when a woman gives birth. A woman can do everything on her own."

I cried when I heard her saying those words, I cried because she's been forced to work while caring me inside, and all my other siblings, until the last minute. I cried for her force and courage, and I felt so guilty for making her go through all that alone. I couldn't understand why I had come into this world when I wasn't desired, for what purpose?

My parents had no clue about the gender of their tenth child as they didn't know of the first nine or the last one. There was no such thing as the amniotic fluid test. Only in science fiction books. It would not have changed anything, my parents were very religious people and abortion was considered a crime, thus a sin.

I came into the world screaming and kicking, and my mother got to be the first to know I was her seventh girl. 'My man won't be happy, he wanted a boy. What can we do? God makes happen whatever is already the plan for us. He's got no choice than to accept this girl,' thought my mother in her head.

I was a big, loud, girl with blue eyes that everybody expected will change colour in time. They didn't. Two days after my birth, my mother was asked what name should be written on the certificate. That moment my mother realised that she had no name in mind. My siblings usually helped her with that task, but whole my family hoped I was a boy. Nobody thought I would turn up a girl. My mother said she'll think about it and let them know as soon as possible. She had worked her brains out for hours, without success. She ran out of girl names. Understandable.

Then something happened. The midwife in charge was ill that day, therefore a replacement had to be provided because women gave birth every day in my village. An external midwife was in that day, and she had a baby boy of the age of three, approximately. As the midwife was checking on my mother, the little boy decided I was his sister and insisted with his mother to remain with me for a while. My mother said he stared at me for hours. He observed my mother breastfeeding me and every time I started crying he did his best to soothe me. He was mesmerised. God knows why because I don't think I was beautiful at the age of two days. I must have looked like a batrachian (frog), but hey, love is blind.

When the midwife's shift ended, she came for the baby boy. But he didn't want to go away from me, so when his mother grabbed him by force, he's started kicking and shouting in despair, "I want my sister to come home with me. Mum, let's take Cristina home, please! She is my sister, and I love her."

A very long dispute took place in there, many emotions were shared. The boy was sobbing for me while I was crying because I heard him yelling. It is well known that crying is contagious and not only among children. On the other hand, both mothers were having fun while watching the scene.

"Would you believe this, Maria, my baby boy, fell in love with your daughter. We should arrange a marriage right now," the midwife said to my mother. They both laughed.

Anyway, when my mother heard the name *Cristina* shouted out loud by that baby boy, she decided it was a sign from God himself. "Cristina will be your name as it was written for you," said my mother's while feeding me. I was quite a hungry infant it appears.

Many times I thought of searching for this boy and thank him for spending some time with my mother when she most needed a human touch and for giving me the name I love immensely. I feel that I owe this human being a great deal of debt. I hope to find him one day and give him at least a hug.

Three years after I was born, my mother received a *Certificate of Maternal Glory*—first degree—signed by the president himself, which stated, "For the merit of having given birth and raised nine children." Although she had another child after me, he didn't count as *raised* because was only one year old at that time. My late brother wasn't included either.

Along with the certificate, my mother received an amount of money. How much I don't know exactly. We had money without that *prize*, but there was nothing to spend them on. That was one of the many paradoxes of the communist regime.

My mother was also in line for a *Heroine Mother Diploma* because she had in fact raised ten children but the decree and laws have changed in the meanwhile. When women have learned that the state will pay a price if you had more than eight children, many decided to give birth to as many children as possible. Naturally, that was to cost the state a very high amount of money, so the Diplomas were forever cancelled. Poor women and especially poor children who came into this world with a promise of cash. No mother got their hands on any of these Certificates or Diplomas ever again after the one my mother received.

The social life in my village

During the communist period, there weren't many shops around. We had three in my village, a small grocery shop; one sold clothing, shoes, and furniture; and the last one was really tiny and had a mix of the two.

There were also two pubs which were full every evening and all day on Sundays. It was an encountering place. All men in the village gathered in there to debate... I actually have no idea about what! No one was allowed to speak about politics. There was a real danger to disappear without a trace if you dared to say anything negative about Communism or the leaders. There were no positives unless you were a candidate in politics. What else could men speak about? Women, hunting, parties? Out of discussion in that period. Men and women knew only work. A very peculiar period of modern slavery, especially for farmers.

There were no programmes on the black and white TVs, except for the evenings, plus Sundays when, the only channel owned by the state, transmitted some shows following a very strict timetable. The broadcasting started around 7:20 pm with the national anthem followed by five minutes of cartoons, made in Romania. Then was one hour of news which showed our leaders going around the country to witness its incredible growing. After that, each evening continued with two distinct shows, one was regarding a problem in the country, electric energy for example "a national issue of every each of us;" another one was a national or international movie, theatre, folk music, or documentary. On Saturdays, the programme started at 6 pm, Sundays around 2 pm with a sort of real-life events from villages. Children had their hour of fame too. We were all pioneers, young future communists, and well-rounded adult communists.

Our favourite show was on Saturday evening, *Tele-Encyclopaedia,* a documentary about the sea life with Jacques-Yves Cousteau. I guess that was the only real and true life we ever been allowed to learn about.

Love was taboo. The intimacies in movies were censored, not even a hug or a kiss on a forehead was ever shown.

There were never discussions about any religion. There was no Easter, no Christmas, and no Santa Claus.

Everything showed on TV was a masquerade. The history taught in school was a lie. We were utterly unaware of what was really going on in the country or in the world. Not that we ever questioned or had any idea of any of the above.

We only knew about rules, laws, duties, how amazing our leaders were, and how incredibly lucky we were to be under that communist regime. We had no idea, back then, that they were indoctrinating us. I thought the rest of the world was exactly in our situation.

When Ceausescu was in visits to some city or village, all population had to be gathered to meet him and his wife. Flags, placards, smiles, enthusiasm, clapping, cheering, traditional costumes were a must. These meetings were long ahead planned, and you had a free day (or half a day) from work or school.

You were not allowed to be ill or about to give birth to a child, you had to be there. No matter what.

To be honest, from what I remember people were actually happy to have a free day from work so, when they got there, everybody was incredibly exuberant. People had to shout various slogans like "Viva Ceausescu! Viva the Communism Party!" at regular intervals, often prompted by a person from Ceausescu's staff. Everything was filmed and shown on TV every day.

Ceausescu loved travelling and visiting. He thought the country was doing amazingly well. Several stories are going around about how people from his staff used to prepare the land where he was foreseen with extreme care. If he wanted to see how apple trees were doing, people were required to take apples from other trees and attach them with a thread to the trees the president was expecting to have a look at. He only saw the trees carefully prepared for his inspection.

The same delicate operation took place with the corn fields. If a regular plant of corn could have had mostly one ear of corn, sometimes two (different sizes), all the plants Ceausescu saw had at least three huge ears of corn. Once again, people worked for days to attach these ears to the plant and make it look real.

Every time we saw these meetings on televisions, we had no doubt that those apple trees were a miracle of God because of the number of perfect fruits they had on their branches. Same with the corn plants. As farmers, we were incredibly amazed and envious of their harvest.

Due to all these tricks, I am inclined to believe that

Ceausescu was somehow kept in the dark from the real situation in the country. But of course, it is only my opinion.

How can anyone think that people could be happy and cheery when they don't have electricity in the house, no oil to cook and no bread to eat?

Rationalised food in the Golden Epoch

In 1981 Romania had to request the International Monetary Fund a line of credit and adopted a policy to pay back its debts. If before Romanians were okay with Ceausescu's dictatorship, that year they all started to feel pressured, used and dispensable. The food began to be rationalised, the power cuts were happening every day, same as the hot running water and central heating, no imports just export. The country was in total austerity, and the president couldn't care less. He had everything he needed and much more.

My family was doing fairly well, much better than others. That because we all worked night and day, no matter what. We had the necessary food for surviving, but chocolates and fruits were a luxury. And when you know you can't have something you want it even more.

The piece of land we had was reserved to growing vegetables. We couldn't afford to plant any sort of tree or grapes. Our neighbours had apple, pear, plum, cherry trees, and several types of grapes and we wanted so badly to have some too, but my father was against it because fruits were not considered nourishment, but a caprice. We exchanged some corn for apples or pears, but that was about it. We terribly craved for cherries and grapes every Autumn.

The first time I saw a banana I was seven maybe. My mother cut it into thin slices and when I tasted one, I thought was very disgusting and refused to eat more.

As I said, there was no chocolate to be found in the two shops of my village. Sometimes my older siblings would bring us some imported from Russia, bought illegally from people in the streets. It was the worst thing I tried in my whole existence back then. It had the exact texture and taste of plasticine. I promise. I tried plasticine when I was in kindergarten, not sure why, but that's how I know what Russian chocolate tasted like. Nobody liked it, not even the birds we raised.

Ironically, twenty kilometres away from my village was a huge chocolate factory, and one of my neighbours worked there. He used to bring home large cubes of raw chocolate, and something else called *glucose*. A sort of raw sugar used in the making of chocolate. His children always vaunt themselves with that, and we were quite envious.

We had loads of milk, cream, and made cheese every day. Every Saturday, my mother baked the most amazing sweet cheese pies in the world. All my siblings were raised in fear of God, and we've been taught that giving is one way to demonstrate you had a good heart, so we always shared our goods with everybody, especially with these neighbours of ours. They were truly poor and in need. However, they never gave us a piece of chocolate or glucose in return. I used to cry and complain with my parents, and my father would always say, "Cristinuza, sweets are not good for your teeth, health nor mind. You have the best food anyone could ever dream, be grateful for that and leave them alone. You don't need their stuff."

"But I give them cheese, and bread, and pies because they are always hungry and their parents never cook. Why can't they share some of their things with us? Why are them this way, Papa?" I would ask with tears in my eyes.

"People are all different, child. Don't be upset. God will always take care of us." My father will reply with sadness.

And when somebody reminded me of God, I would just fall in adoration as I was a true believer.

Anyway, my uncle used to bring us chocolates from time to time, proper and amazing chocolate, but I wanted glucose. That was the only sweet I ever liked as a child.

***

My family didn't know what vegetarianism was back then. We had no idea that there were people in the world who wouldn't eat meat, eggs, or cheese. We survived on these aliments. We raised many chickens, geese, turkeys, bunnies, pigs, and our father took care of cows for a living, and with the vegetables we grew on the land, we had absolutely everything you can think of. But all these animals, land and the slavery required loads of hard work. That's why every each of us did their part for the well-being of the family. Which meant we never had any spare time to play with other children. In fact, I have only random memories about this kind of activity.

But no matter how much food we had in the winter, there were some types of food we didn't have in the summer time. That because the meat or sausages were delicate and not having a fridge was quite a limitation. During the winter my mother used to cook all the meat in fat pigs and conserve it in huge jars. However, in the late summer, most of it was finished.

Therefore, we were constrained to go in the city to look for products from meat, especially when there was a big celebration close, like a village feast.

As I said, the food was rationalised, and there wasn't much to buy from the shops in my village anyway. Only some of the vital aliments like oil, bread, sugar, rice, and some sweets like biscuits and candies. A day a week in the summer time, one sold ice cream.

Families were given a ration book, and farmers were required to give to the state a percentage of all their goods. For example, if they had ten chickens, one had to be delivered to the shop when they went to buy the rationed food for the month. If they had hens, twenty eggs belonged to the state and so on. This was supposed to happen every four months. Not sure what kind of calculations were made and based on what. What I do know is that this didn't happen in the cities, but only in the rural areas. How did they know that you had or not? Well, at the beginning of each year, a census of people and everything they owned took place. You could have tried to lie or hide your birds or pigs, but random inspections were made and it they found something you omitted to mention, much more, or everything you had would have been taken away from you. It didn't matter you'd said that three of your chickens died or were stolen, or that you had to feed your children.

***

I remember once when my mother didn't have the last egg to take to the shop and the vendor refused to give her the rationed food for that month. My mother cried, begged, and promised she will bring the egg the next month because the hens made none in the last month. The vendor not only remained unwavering but insulted her in countless ways. She came home humiliated, crying her heart out. She was utterly desperate because she had no oil to cook dinner that evening.

I kneeled at her feet, held her hand and tried to calm her down but I couldn't. We both cried until no tears were left inside us. It was then I swore that I will do everything in my power and never allow anyone to mock my mother again.

The next day, my mother went to one of her sisters and begged for an egg, then went back to the shop and brought home the 100 millilitres per capita of sunflower oil, the rice, and the sugar. I wished we didn't have to eat so my mother wouldn't have had to bow her head in front of heartless humans.

I sometimes thought that it was better to have nothing because your ration would still have been given to you regardless. The more you had, the more you were required to give. By logic, if you had more, was because you worked more. But that didn't count.

Allow me to remind you (and me too) what the theory of Communism is, "a system of social organisation in which all property is owned by the community, each person contributes and receives according to their ability and needs." - Wikipedia

All my family, from children to elderly, worked for twenty hours a day to ensure we all had food on the table in each day of our lives. Some people had no idea of what work was, individuals who drank and slept the whole day but had same quantities of rationed food anyway.

In the cities, people had jobs and paid taxes, but that was about it. My mother worked on her land for the country, received no money in return, and was forced to share her chickens with the state. Moreover, in villages, you couldn't find milk, eggs, any product made from meat, chocolate, toys, or fruits. Left aside the fact you couldn't find clothes, shoes, shampoo, or soap.

When the harvest of grain was good, we baked bread once or twice a week, but there were years in which the state kept everything for itself, so we were forced to buy bread. I wasn't so fond of bread, I preferred polenta a thousand times more; however, cold polenta in the winter time wasn't that delicious. At home, we were able to make fresh polenta at any time, but my father needed to have lunch at work—he left the house every morning at 4 or 5 am and came back at 7 pm—therefore, a piece of bread was a must.

They didn't sell bread every day in our village shop. I don't know if it was because farmers were supposed to have grain or corn and bake their own bread, or because nobody gave a damn on us. Usually, when the rumours reached my family that on a certain day bread was expected to be sold in the village, my mother used to send me to stay in line and buy at least two loaves (of 270 or 320 grams each). Because we were eight siblings and two parents, two loaves were a joke, but it was better than nothing. We treated it as a delicacy.

Nobody knew the exact time of the day the bread will get there, so people would wait for hours in an Indian queue in front of the shop. However, when the vendor would open the doors to let us in, all that order became a total chaos in a matter of seconds. Every time. I was just a child, 5-11 years old, but the others were strong adolescent males. I was often pushed aside or thrown on the ground and stepped on with no mercy. Most of the time, even if I was the first one in the queue, in one second I would become the last, and I would cry, beg and shout in despair. A fight for life and death because I knew there weren't enough loaves for everyone. The thought of going home empty handed terrified me. That would have resulted in no lunch for my father for the next day. I couldn't stand that. I didn't want my father to suffer hunger when he worked for so many hours a day. It was the least I could do for him.

One day they started to sell two loaves per person in the queue, and I was euphoric. Usually, they only sold one. My heart was racing from a mix of excitement and fear. I was afraid that the bread will end before I got the chance to buy any. I was praying all Gods in the universe, as every time I was in a queue; however, when it got my turn, the vendor decided to sell me only one piece. With tears on my cheeks, I complained right away asking for two, as the person in front of me, "I have got seven siblings at home, plus my parents. It is not fair."

Do you know what the vendor did? He refused to sell me any because I was too *arrogant*.

Luckily, people were on my side and joined me in the protest, "Give her two loaves, she's a part of the most numerous family in the village. One will never be enough. Don't you have a soul?" The vendor knew me very well because I was often seen with my mother, but he couldn't care less. To be honest, I am sure he didn't like any of my family members and did that on purpose. However, when everybody started to shout at him, he had no choice than giving me two and let me go. I went outside with the dress tore apart and full of bruises, but with happiness inside my soul. "I did it! I did it!" I shouted with pride, hugged the loaves, and ran home as fast as I could. That was a lucky day for me, and we didn't have many during that period.

That happened in the village, but in the cities, they sold more than two loaves, and you didn't need a ration book for it. Back then, because bread was made from wholemeal, most people thought they were only good to feed the pigs. Personally, I preferred it to the white bread, like all my other siblings. My father was never bothered of what he ate unless it was cold polenta which he never liked. My mother's favourite was the white bread, but she was alone in that.

Going to the city required to buy a bus ticket, more money to spend and not all people in the village were willing to do that. We needed bread in order to survive, especially when there was a scarcity of flour in our reserves, my mother would ask me if I wanted to go and buy at least ten or fifteen loaves at one time. And with that occasion, I always went and brought to my sister some potatoes and random vegetables of the period. I was just a child and ten kilogrammes of potatoes were extremely heavy, but I never said no. Not even because I was utterly terrified to travel by bus. If I had to be at school by 8 am, I would wake up at 4 am and take the first bus into the city. From there I would first go and leave the heavy bags at my sister's place. I needed at least thirty minutes to get there, and from there I would run like the best athlete in the world, get into the first shop, buy as many loaves they would sell me, then search for another one, and buy others until I had no more space in my two huge bags. Luckily, fifteen loaves of bread were not as heavy as ten kilogrammes of potatoes.

The last step was the shop in the bus station. In there they always sold me as many loaves I wanted, if I had the money. I could have run from my sister's place to there without a stop, but I was never sure I would find any bread in there. Sometimes there was none left, and it happened to me once. I had to go back into the city to look for bread in other shops and missed the bus to the village. After that, I could have never taken the chance to buy all the necessary bread from there. But I always checked, even if my bags were full. On that period, the plastic bags were rare as gold. My uncle left some to us, and I used to carry one with me all the time, just in case. When the shop from the bus stop had bread, I'd spent all the money I had left on my last bread of the day. My mother was always so happy when I got home with fifteen or twenty loaves. That meant we could all have as much bread as we felt like for almost a week. We didn't have butter or margarine, those were delicacies, and we only bought some to make cakes or cookies for special days. However, we had quince or apple jam to spread on top of it. Not only that, my father exchanged milk with a sort of dark wine marmalade which we loved immensely. What a treat for all of us.

Meat, sausages, bacon, generally meat products were not that easy to find in the city close to us. For that, we needed to get up at 2:30 – 3:00 am, walk for six kilometres on foot and travel for at least seventy by train. I was a very strong, resourceful, and resilient child but that trip was too dangerous to be made alone; therefore, my mother would always send me when at least two other adults would express their desire to go to that city with the same reason as mine. Many times I came home with nothing in my bag, completely exhausted and disappointed. My mother never got upset. It wasn't my fault in the end, she knew that I always did my best in everything. If my bag was empty, it meant that there was no meat at all anywhere.

What's been bothering me for all these years is how come that period was called *The Golden Epoch*? Who gave it this name? Based on what? The dictator's style of life?

School, pioneers, and books

Going to school was compulsory in my country, thank God for that! All Ceausescu's speeches contained the following slogan borrowed from Lenin, "Study, Study, and Study again."

However, this maxim wasn't addressed to farmers' children. The country survived on agriculture. Farmers were not really required to go to school, just on the land. But nobody ever made this distinction in public. The Communism's theory was that we all had the same rights.

For many children going to school was a burden, for me was the best thing in the whole world and I loved it with all my heart. From a very early age instead of playing, I sat in the corner of the bed and watched my older sisters writing or reading. I could not understand how anyone can create a word from nothing, then phrases from words, furthermore, entire stories from phrases. It seemed a sorcery back then, and I was absolutely fascinated. I envied them so badly, and I couldn't wait to be able to do it myself.

It is common practice for children to be taught writing and reading as soon as possible. Some are starting at the age of two, and by the time they reached five they already know how to put words onto paper. Not me, and not my little brother. I don't know about my older siblings. I guess it was tradition in my country not to do the educators' job. They didn't teach that in the kindergarten, we had to be six to go to school and learn the secret of knowledge. But

I couldn't wait any longer, and in July of 1981, I started asking my mother to send me to school.

After my little brother's birth, my mother was diagnosed with a heart disease. As a result, she wasn't able to go to work the land every single day as always. So when she was home, in the morning before going to kindergarten, then in the afternoon, in the evening, and before going to be, I would say these words over and over again, "Mum, please, send me to school. I want to be able to read as my older siblings." She would look funny at me and laugh at first, but when I started to beg and shed countless tears, my mother took me seriously and went to speak with the school director. Unfortunately, there were rules, you must have turned six before the 14th of September, the new scholastic year, to be accepted in school. I was born in the middle of November, so I was five years and ten months old. Too young.

I was devastated by the news, and I cried, kicked and pulled my hair out. I ran away in the garden, rolled my body into a ball and sobbed for hours until my father came home and tried to take me inside by force. I didn't want to give up, and I kept insisting. Then I stopped eating, and my parents worried. I heard them discussing the situation, and many harsh words were spoken. My mother said she already tried, my father demanded her to try again and she started crying, "Why don't you go to speak with him? You are her father; your name is respected, and your words have more weight. You always let me deal with the education of our children, it is not fair. I cannot do everything on my own."

"I cannot miss a day of work; we need the money to buy things for the other four children who are about to start a new scholastic year in a while."

My mother was crying, and my little brother didn't understand what was going on, so he started sobbing too. I felt so guilty for have been the cause of those countless fights between my parents. It was heart-breaking witnessing to such a habitual scene. I sat in the corner of the living room and joined them in the weeping. My father couldn't stand the sight of such emotions and demanded us to stop. It was easier said than done. We went to bed with our eyes inundated by tears, like many other nights before.

A week after, I asked again, and my mother had a brilliant idea. She brought my little brother into consideration, "Who'll take Sebastian to kindergarten? He's still too young to go and stay alone in there. Plus, the best teacher in the village will start a new generation of students next year. It's in your best interest to wait another year."

I cried again, but my mother had put on the table very valid arguments. Besides, there was nothing anyone can do. Too many children in the village. Each generation had four classes of thirty-two students, there wasn't a single free place. I had to accept it and move on. I wanted so badly to be able to read and write, but nobody even considered to teach me the alphabet's letters at home. Or maybe they did consider it, but nobody ever mentioned it though. Everybody was busy with their studies, the chores around the house, and on the land.

At the end of August, my mother went into town to buy uniforms for my older siblings, two boys, and two girls. Four of my other siblings, all girls, were already moved out my parents' house. Three of them were married, the other one was going to a boarding school.

I was envious and heartbroken, but there was nothing anyone could do.

***

I went to school in 1982, when the country was in total despair.

In August that year, my mother went to stay in an endless queue to buy me all the necessary for school, pencils, erasers, crayons, block notes, drawing blocks, various books. I was so excited and kept running on the street to see my mother coming with the bags full of those wonders of which I have dreamed for years. She came home five hours later, completely exhausted. That shop was just twenty minutes away. It was normal, so nobody complained.

When my mother gave me the heavy bag, I started crying from emotion. I couldn't believe that I was soon to become a student. I opened it and looked through everything. I touched every object, smelled it, and thought I was the luckiest child in the whole universe. What I liked most was the black fountain pen. Back then, it was compulsory to write with the fountain pens. Regular pens were prohibited. I really don't know why. My mother asked me to be careful with it not only because was expensive, but mostly because they couldn't be found anywhere until the following year.

Then my mother went to the city and bought my first uniform. A dress with small blue and white squares, plus a blue sort of apron, both made from cotton.

I was so in love that everybody thought I was completely out of my mind. No child was happier and eager to go to school than me. My family took me for a freak, but I didn't care.

I loved the first day of school, even if I was all shaky and terrified. The school had three distinct buildings in its precincts. The oldest one was reserved for the primary school, the newest for the secondary, and another in between for the college and library. The rooms had no central heating, and the school had no science laboratories or computers.

The bathroom was a separate building with no running water. But I was happy, and I didn't know children around the world had better conditions. I was living a dream and I have always been all eyes and ears during the classes. I wouldn't have missed a minute of it, ever, under no circumstances. I promised that I will go to school dead or alive. Best period of my life.

The letters were a miracle. We learned a new one every day, and in less than a month I was able to read and write without any help. I thought I would die from happiness. My first dream came true! Because my voice was clear and powerful, the teacher, Maria, used to ask me to read for the class every day. I didn't like that at all, but I always listened and did what was asked of me.

Then I went to the library and borrowed my first book, *Les miserable*, by Victor Hugo. The librarian thought I was too young for such a book, but I insisted and promised I will give up reading it if I couldn't understand what was all about in the first ten pages. Do you think I could let that book off my hands until I finished it? Yes, I left it because I still went to help my siblings and my mother on the land, I still helped with the chores in and around the house. I kept feeding the pigs, the birds and continued cooking. But when the night came, and the lights were switched off, that's a metaphor because the lights were already off from the dictator's decision, I would go into my room, light a candle and moved into a different world. I cried so much and felt the pain of those poor children. I wished I could help them... but who was helping me?

When I took the book back, three days later, the librarian was quite impressed. At least it's what I thought until a few months later when she proved me wrong. After that first book, I asked if I could have two books at once. I didn't have much time to go to the library. She wasn't very happy, but gave them to me, but not after I promised I would actually read them and not go through the pictures only. I didn't understand what she meant with that.

I took the books back in three days again, she looked at me with scepticism, but still gave me the other two books I asked for. My new favourite author was another illustrious French name, Jules Verne. I devoured his books with incredible fervour. The worlds he transported me in were absolutely magical. They were incredibly easy and fast to read. The next time I dared to ask for three books at once. The librarian refused categorically. I begged and promised I will take them back on time. When she denied my request again, I brought to the table that she just lent three books to another student. "I saw it with my eyes minutes ago. You cannot be so unfair towards me," I cried.

"Child, that student is in the secondary, you're in the primary! Do you see why I am so reluctant to lend you so many books at once?" explained the librarian.

"I promised I can handle them. They are easy

books, and I am a very fast reader. Please! I won't leave this room without these three books."

She had no choice but giving them to me. "But you don't have to bring them back in three days, take your time. You have two weeks. Okay?" shouted the librarian after I grabbed the books and ran outside the darkroom.

I was holding those books as they were the most precious thing I ever had in my hands, and I was immensely happy. I thought I could do anything when I was reading.

When I took them back, five days later, the librarian made me sit and interrogated me about the content of all of them. Only then I realised that the look in her eyes wasn't positive. I answered all her questions, and she was still not convinced.

"It's hard for me to believe that a child could read so many books in five days. Do you do your homework? What are your parents saying when they see you bringing home all these books?" asked the librarian.

"I just love reading, I do my homework every day. I don't miss a day of school because I love studying. As for my parents, they don't know I read, they think I study. They are very severe and strict about learning and being good in school. I am a good student, you can ask my teacher, Maria, if you don't believe me. She'll tell you everything about me." I omitted to mention that I was also helping with the chores in and around the house, with the land, and my mother with the weaving. She would have definitely thought that I was lying or maybe she would have accused my parents of exploiting me. Which wasn't true at all. I was the one offering all the time.

I was indeed a good student, and my teacher was very fond of me. I always had fantastic grades, and I was among the elite in the class. However, at the end of the year, when I was expecting a first or second prize, along with my parents, at the very last minute, it was given to somebody else. A student, two or three students who weren't supposed to have any prize whatsoever. I never cared, but my parents felt very humiliated and discriminated. We all knew why. Corruption and blackmail were very popular in my country. During those times if a powerful parent went to a teacher and asked them to give their child a prize, although they didn't deserve it, the teacher had to agree. For a reason or another. Maybe an amount of money was put on the table, maybe offers of favours or even menaces.

One year, I don't remember if it was the first or the second, or even the third grade, the teacher came to me and asked for forgiveness because she had no prize for me although I deserved it. She was in such distress. I am not sure how I reacted because I don't have any memories after her confession. Maybe I was too upset and imposed my mind to forget, as I did with many other bad experiences in my life, just to be able to move on and forgive. But I don't think I was too upset, just very disappointed.

She's long gone now, may she rest in peace, and I don't have anything against her. I genuinely loved her despite the fact she gave my prizes away. She always showed me that she cared and was good enough for me.

We all went to school, my parents were very strict about it, especially my father. Under no circumstances, any of us would stay home from school. Ever. Unless you were, of course, very ill. But we were all quite healthy children mostly because the food we ate was free of chemicals and we also spent loads of time outside, under the sunshine, running wild and filling our lungs with fresh air. Our brain was very well oxygenated at any time of the year, as you can imagine. All my siblings were born with quite a quantity of intelligence. They were fast thinkers and learners, therefore set as examples to follow. The only thing that we were missing was confidence, so it was very rare that we would raise our hands to give a correct answer when educators and teachers asked the class. Luckily, some of them were very good at understanding human behaviour and would call our names to provide the answer when nobody else has come up with one. We've never failed to impress them, but it wasn't enough to exceed in a world of discrimination and censures.

I loved helping my family with everything I could, but I also loved school. It was a parallel universe, and I never missed a day. Maths, grammar, literature, and languages were my favourite classes. Nowadays, children around the world learn to read and write at a very young age, three, four, five or even earlier. I learned all these at seven. My parents tacitly empowered my older siblings with the education of the youngest generations but didn't have time to teach me.

***

Everybody was a communist when my mother gave birth to me, but you weren't born into it. Nevertheless, there was no choice; nobody asked you if you wanted to be one or not.

I remember the day I became part of Romania's

pioneer movement (future communists) with all my colleagues. I was at the elementary, eight years of age. The date was prefixed by the school, and we were all very emotional. I had no idea of what I was doing back then, it was required and considered an honour, that's what we've been told. We had an asseveration ceremony, and red cravats with our country flag on the borders of it were given to us. They even rewarded us with a school day trip, paid by our parents, though, which weren't very happy about it. We went to visit the Neamt Citadel, a medieval fortress built in the 14th century. Restored in 2007, it looks quite impressive now but back then they were just some ruins, and I could not understand why we were there, to see what exactly? To be honest, there is a rich and important history about it, but my interest in history wasn't very deep.

The trip was a tradition, every new generation of pioneers visited the same place.

I thought my father was a communist, my mother too, but it wasn't quite the same for them as they weren't students when the king was forced to abdicate in the favour of Populism or Communism. They were still children, but because of the Second World War, they had no school to go to; therefore, they weren't proudly invested as pioneers. My father wasn't an actual farmer as he had a day job in the city. In there he was approached and tempted by an offer of money to become a Communist Party member, but he didn't accept it. Refusing to become an active communist was considered treason, and you could have lost your freedom and your life in one instant.

My father was a man with strong principles and couldn't betray them. As he was a very hard and reliable worker, plus a respected father, his rare case was not brought to the attention of the men in power; hence he never had a communist ID.

My mother was never asked or offered to become a member of the Communism Party as she was just a farmer. Her participation would have never counted for anything. Farmers were not deserving, farmers were slaves.

I didn't even know there was anyone in the country not being a communist. I never questioned this, and my parents never spoke about it; it was just an assumption I made.

Children were required to help the adults at the collective (all the land took from the owners and put together). Every new scholastic year started with a period of hard work for all students, no matter the age. It wasn't an option; you had to go and gather onions, potatoes, tomatoes, corn and so on. Whatever needed to be done first.

The parents sent the children to school, and the school sent the students on the fields. My father would always get upset when hearing such barbarity. This happened in villages and maybe only in my region. I really don't know. What I do know is that my assistance was required to help reach the targets. It was a rule of the Communist government, one of many. Gifted with a deep sense of duty I've never complained when coming back from school I was expected to take care of the house, feed the animals and work on the land for the family or the state. It didn't seem unfair or outrageous to me, on the contrary, I felt I was doing my duty. To be honest, I always offered, since I can remember. It was the least I could do. Someone had to do it. If my other siblings were busy with studying, I would just step in and do whatever needed to be done to the best of my ability.

One day, when I was six, they were debating who was going to stay home and cook dinner. I have a sister who wasn't very fond of cooking, so she would always try her best to persuade someone else to do it for her. That day I said I'll do it. They all looked at me in disbelief. I was a little too young to cook for eight people (two of my older sisters were already married and had their children at that time). I was asked if I had ever cooked before.

"No, but I can do it. I watched mum doing it. It's no big deal," I said convinced.

"All right then, it is settled. Give it a go," they said unwillingly. There was a lot to be done in the fields that day, in all honesty, they had no choice as I was really too small to deal with the quantity of the production expected to be delivered that day.

I gave it a go, so to speak. I didn't do an exceptional job but trust me when I tell you that I was very happy for have been trusted with the cooking as I was very passionate about it. I cooked potatoes with meat and a huge polenta. I wasn't tall enough to reach the stove and stir the food, so I put a wooden box under my feet. It worked perfectly. The dinner was ready when my siblings came home from the fields, and they were all quite impressed. Same as my father and my mother who came home much later than all. We might all have been asleep by that time. I don't even remember seeing her every day.

My father looked at me in wonder and told me to be careful not to set the house on fire next time. The stove worked with wood, but we didn't have much during the Communism as we preserved our trees and forests, therefore we used corn cobs or the whole plant dried. It was a cheap and fast way to cook, but also dirty and very dangerous. It required constant attention. So, yes, it was demanding, but I never ran away from tough tasks.

My mother's art

There were four seasons in my country, all very clearly delimited by the weather. During each of them, the land had to go through various stages of production.

I start with the winter, my favourite season. It used to snow a lot, and the temperatures would always drop around minus thirty Celsius degrees. You might think that during this period farmers would rest and charge their batteries for the next year of hard work, and you are right. Most farmers were doing just that, except a few families like mine. We didn't go to play in the snow making snowmen as our mother never stopped working every single day of the year, except Sundays—God's day. She was a handloom weaver. There were a few women in the village doing the same, but she was a true artist, The Best. You might think I am biased, but you'd change your mind if you saw my mother's work. Hundreds of rugs weaved by her hands were sold in the markets, thousands of metres of different styles of tapestries are to be found in several houses in my village and not only. She earned a degree of fame in that period. People would come from far away to buy a rug made by my mother as her work would stand out from thousands. Her artwork was easy on the eyes and filled people's heart with joy. Every piece was impeccable, each colour was perfectly balanced, and no mistake was ever to be found in any of them.

She was a perfectionist and would have never finished a piece knowing it was a mistake in it. If the fault wasn't captured until the very end, she would unweave every centimetre to get there and fixed it. Unweaving takes a considerable amount of energy and quadruples the time. The flaw might have been invisible to everybody's eyes, but not hers. She would spot one from several metres away.

My mother never rested during the winter when the land was frozen, so we couldn't either because she needed the thread and wool prepared, ready to be used for the rugs. Wool was easy to find and set up but had terrible faults. First, moths loved it; secondly, the colour would wash off very easily, therefore my mother would only work with synthetic wool. This had brighter and forever stable colours plus an impressive durability. A piece, which would take my mother four or five months of daily work, was going to remain intact and eternal.

We, children, after doing the homework, were assigned to prepare the thread, forming perfect clews of wool. The five months of winter would go by like that every year. Personally, I loved every single day of it.

The snow covered everything with thick layers, sometimes three or four metres of fluffy and cold white material. The view was breathtaking. Pure magic. Never seen anything more idyllic than that in my life.

We went to school walking on the snow, then coming home, completely frozen got changed and sit around the terracotta stove listening to the crackling fire and my mother's weaving. The whole family united was heaven on earth for me. Priceless memories.

***

When the snow started to melt, spring would hesitantly settle in. Every snowdrop's birth indicated the time has come for the land to be ploughed and sown.

Most farmers were anxious to go out after a long period of lethargy. As we never rested, we were already tired.

***

When summer showed up, the young plants needed weeding. This process was very demanding and required certain skills, caring and patience as it had to be done at least two times consecutively. You would finish weeding all the land you had once, then you had to start all over again because the weed would grow faster than the plants. You couldn't afford to omit the second weeding as the production would tremendously drop, at the point that you wouldn't have a harvest period because there was nothing fully matured.

This was valid only for the piece of land exploited for your family survival. The state wouldn't control what you've done on your crop, it was your own business.

My family, for example, divided the soil situated behind the house, in many small crops. Every single metre was destined for growing a specific vegetable, herb, corn, or potato.

We had no flowers and no fruit trees, we couldn't afford any waste of fertile soil. Trees were growing big, and their branches would have prevented the sunlight to caress the crops. We had no idea that there were fruit trees that don't grow big back then.

We loved fruits a lot, especially cherries and grapes, but fruits were not considered food (as I said before), and although we've asked and cried to have at least an apple tree planted, my father decision was final. If there was something I really missed, was a tree fruit. I had many dreams about this for years.

Flowers were out of the question, no discussion allowed. Ever.

***

September was the start of Autumn. The Schools would open for a new year of studying and all the work done during the whole year on the land would finally show their fruits. Every single farmer, from an early age, was required to help with the harvest. Many parents were very protective of their children and never expected them to do such a demanding job, but the government had a different opinion, "Children need to be taught to do everything and take care of themselves as soon as they got rid of the diapers. It's for their own good."

I must admit that I agree to that now, as I agreed back then, still, most of the time we were forced to work for several hours without fresh water or a break. Many were crying from fatigue and dehydration, but the schools had to give their contribution for the greater good. Students had to help finish the harvest. No matter what, no excuse. But only the students from villages were submitted to this sort of treatment. As I said, people living in the cities had no land to give to the state and work on. They had jobs in the factories, and that was their contribution. Except they were paid to do it, were entitled to holidays and free days, and when the time has come for them to retire, they would have a good pension to live from.

From my experience, farmers were deprived of their properties and forced into slavery. They weren't paid in money but were given a percentage of the whole year production. If the year was poor, you didn't receive anything. Farmers were given the permission to retire at least five years later than the factory people, and their pension was a joke. No person was able to survive on that money.

Please forgive me for reminding you again what Communism is, "each person contributes and receives according to their abilities and needs."

Autumn Harvest

I've never liked Autumn. For a farmer, it is the most demanding season. Both physically and psychologically. The weather was bad, it rained a lot, and the unpaved roads of all villages were full of mud and puddles. The days were shorter, and the sun stopped to shine. It was cold, windy, and dark. People were always in the fields, completely drained of energy.

Women were also in charge of making jams and various canned vegetable stews for the winter. The legume and vegetable production had to be conserved for the long winter to come. We had no fridge if you remember.

Farmers were working incessantly with little sleep. Children were going to school from where they were taken into the fields to help the *Collective* with the last step in the agriculture system. Nothing could have been postponed no more. It didn't matter it was raining or even snowing, the harvest had to be finished at any cost. There was a lot of pressure from many sides.

I couldn't stand the dirt. I loved the green of the fields and the trees. The dead leaves on the ground were the clear sign that nature was slowly dying. The landscape had a very daunting look. All things were either brown or grey. I felt cold every day, deep down in my bones. Every morning I would go outside, had a look around and started to shiver uncontrollably. Everything and everyone looked utterly miserable.

A Saturday morning, my father woke me up to go

and harvest the beetroots. My mother was ill, my siblings were in charge with our crop from behind the house, so my father took a few days off to help us finishing the work on the land before winter. I was eight maybe, and I didn't have school on weekends. It was still completely dark outside and inside, that's why my father was holding a candle in his hands. I had a quick look at the clock which indicated it was 5: 30 am. "Papa, I am so cold and tired today," I murmured.

"I know, child, I know. But we had to collect the beetroots and send them to the Sugar Factory to be processed. We cannot postpone this any longer. Your mother doesn't feel very well today; we are the only ones who can do this. Hurry up, I'll wait outside," said my father while placing the candle in a glass full or corn flour. "Don't forget to blow on it before you leave, so it won't burn without a purpose."

"Yes, Papa. Don't worry, you know you can trust me."

I looked at my siblings sleeping in various beds in the room, they seemed so peaceful. I moved as slowly as possible, dressed up, blew on the candle and left the room five minutes later.

Outside, I washed my face with fresh cold water from a bucket. We didn't have running water in the house, what we had instead was a fountain, twenty metres deep. We used buckets to take the water out. I am sure you don't have any idea of what I am talking about, as you might have never seen something like that in your life. Anyway, it was quite dangerous for a child to use this fountain. It required strength and a certain height.

My father started coughing, it was a false cough to

make me aware of the fact he was waiting.

"I need to go to the toilet, Papa. I am not a robot."

"Hurry up," he said, "we need to be ready when the cart arrives, there is a lot to do."

"I know that, but I have needs as all beings. You can start walking without me, I'll reach you in about two minutes."

It was cold and windy as every day of the last week. I looked at the sky emptied of stars, 'It's cloudy. I hope it won't rain. God, please, don't let the rain fall today. We need to finish the beetroot harvest.'

My father is way ahead of me, and I started running and reached him one minute later.

"Stop running," he said, "you don't want to hurt yourself. Who'll work the land and help your mother with the house and the weaving?"

"I won't hurt myself," I said and asked myself, 'Is it really only this the reason that my father doesn't want to see me hurt? I refuse to believe that!'

My father was carrying a few things, so I tried to take the sickle and the bag with food and water from his hands. "I will carry them; I am stronger than you. Save your energy for the harvest, you'll need them."

We walked in silence for at least fifty minutes. There was no living soul on the unpaved streets, no animals, no humans. The village was still asleep. I was thinking of the homework I needed to do that weekend, Sunday or maybe that night before going to bed if it wasn't going to be too late.

We finally reached our piece of land. The dawn was settled, and we were able to start working.

"I am hungry, Papa, can I eat something?"

"Why didn't you eat before leaving the house? There is no time!" he snapped out.

"But Papa...." I thought of trying to reason with him, but I knew it was pointless. 'I'll survive,' I said to myself.

Suddenly my father took out a piece of bread from the bag and handed it to me in silence. I grabbed it with tears in my eyes and started chewing on it, holding the bread in one hand and the sickle on the other one. I raised my head and had a long look at the piece of land full of beetroot.

"How long do you think it will take us, Papa? Do you think we'll finish by three in the afternoon like we did last year?"

"That's impossible. You are just a child."

"But last year were just us two again, and it was all done by two in the afternoon, Papa. Why are you always so pessimistic? It's not good, Papa, I have told you so many times."

My father looked at me betraying mix feelings, anger, and wonder. But said nothing, spit on his hands and grabbed the first beetroot by the brown leaves. One second later the beetroot came out of the ground full of brown soil. My father cleaned it up with one hand and used the sickle to cut the leaves off. He then threw it on the earth, three metres ahead of him. It's where we made the first heap of beetroots.

I took another bite of bread and started doing the same. Some beetroots were easy to dig up, others not so much. Twenty minutes later, the first heap was behind us, and we started the second one. Father worked one metre away from me. We didn't speak, just focused on the job. I was all sweaty and breathing heavily. 'Les Miserables we are,' I thought, but didn't say anything.

The sun was out now, and I didn't even notice it for a while. It was hot, and I was thirsty. I looked for the bottle of water, but the bag was quite far away.

"Papa," I shouted, "I am going to bring the water, do you want some?"

He didn't answer so I started running toward the end of the croft. I found the bottle and drank as much as I could. It was already tepid, but I didn't mind. I grabbed all the things and went back fast, giving the bottle to my father. He took it and drank the half of it. He was thirsty too, maybe even dehydrated, but he didn't want to waste time going back to take the bottle from the bag.

"It's warm. Soon we'll have to go and bring some fresh one," he said. Then looked at me and asked how everything was going.

"It's going well. I am positive will finish by the time Uncle John reaches us."

"The harvest is low this year; the beetroots are quite small," my father replied.

"I don't think so, Papa. Last year was much worse, don't always complain. God will punish us by taking it all from us. You know how it works."

His brown eyes were very sad, and my heart was bleeding for him.

"We'll be fine, Papa, don't worry. God will help us, have faith."

"What kind of child are you? How do you know these things? Who's teaching you religion?"

"I read loads of books," I replied. " And when I go to church, I listen carefully."

"You read? When?! You should do your homework, not read! The school is important."

"Reading is learning. I read when I can, in my school breaks..." - 'during the night,' I thought, but I didn't say it out loud as he would have gone ballistic on me.

"You sure are something, child... let's go back to work."

"When will we have lunch? I am hungry again."

"Midday," he looked at the sun and continued, "in about one hour."

"How do you know what time it is? You don't have a watch."

"It's the sun, look carefully. You'll learn to know the hour by looking at the sun as you've learned to read the clock. Remember?"

I didn't reply and went back two years in my memory when my father taught me the time reading. It seemed impossible at first and thought I was never going to learn. Every couple of minutes my father asked what time it was and a few hours later, I knew every each of them. How proud of myself I felt!

"You need to know the time, so you won't be late to school. We'll not always be here to wake you up," he used to say.

I had another long look at the crop trying to understand when we'll be finishing it. I bent again with the sickle in my hand and pulled out with force every single beetroot from my parcel.

"Be careful with that sickle, don't cut yourself, alright?" shouted my father.

I didn't reply as I was in a parallel universe where I was lying on a bench reading thousands of books. Someone called my name from a distance. I was daydreaming and didn't answer. I couldn't come out to reality. I wanted to sit on a bench and read.

"Cristinuza, it's midday, come to eat. Hello? Do you hear me?"

I raised my head and saw my father waving both hands. I had no choice but changing universes. "I am coming," I said while putting down the sickle and walking towards my father. He was holding the bag with food. "Do you know what your mother's prepared for us today?"

"No," I replied. "I hope we have boiled eggs. Mum cooks them to perfection. Not too soft and not too hard. Amazing. I think she's a witch."

I opened the bag and looked inside. I took the small rug from it and put it on the soil so we could sit on it. There was plenty of food, eggs, cheese, polenta, pork. I was very happy while preparing the picnic, as I used to call it.

"Papa, will you sit for a few minutes, please? You need to rest. Fifteen minutes, not more."

"There is no time, I'll stand."

I looked at him with sadness and he changed his mind. He sat and tried to take his black Wellington off, but it was impossible. "Do you want me to help you?" I asked.

"No, it's fine. I don't have to do that. I don't know what I was thinking, it's just midday, not the end of the day!"

"Your feet are on fire I guess. Those boots are like a stove when it's sunny... pity it doesn't feel the same way during the winter."

We were both eating absently. We looked around as other people were doing the same. It was either a tradition or an imitation of one another. I don't know, but it happened all the time. As soon as someone sat for lunch, others were following. Maybe a tacit understanding or a farmer's pact.

It was a very hot day of Autumn and felt like more like Spring. I loved Spring, it was my second favourite after Winter.

I took one boiled egg and opened it with a teaspoon. I was curious to know if my mother's done it again. I was always amazed by her ability to cook eggs to absolute perfection.

I love boiled eggs and tried many times to cook them the way my mother does, but they are always either too hard or very much uncooked. I asked her how she did it once, so she's explained it in detail, "I put cold water in the cauldron, add the eggs and as soon as the water starts boiling, I count to 120 and take them out."

"120?! Why this number?" I asked surprised. "It sounds like a sorcery to me."

"It's no magic, child. 120 are two minutes." That's how my mother taught me.

The egg was once again perfect. I cut a piece of polenta and put a small piece inside the egg. The yolk came out. I licked the shell as I didn't want it to go to waste. It was the best part. My father looked at me in disgust. He didn't like that. He didn't like many things. Eating for him was a necessity. "We need to eat for survival." For me it's a pleasure of life, and I was grateful.

Five minutes later, my father stood up and said he has finished and will go back to work.

"You always do that Papa! We need to rest a little. We are not slaves; you make me feel like one. Please. Look, everybody is having a siesta, some even sleep for a while."

"Don't be silly, it's Saturday. We need to be back

before twilight. Your mother is waiting for you to help her with the washing and cooking."

"But where are the others? Why nobody else came with us? My sisters could help mum with the washing. I am never sure what's going on in this family."

"They need to study and finish the work on our crop," my father replied. "Hurry up, John will soon be here."

"We've almost finished, haven't we? We might have to wait for him. I told you we'll finish on time."

"We still have a lot to do. I am going, you rest if you want."

I would have liked to lay down on the rug for a while, but I couldn't stand watching my father working, or anyone else for that matter. It's one of my many weaknesses. Besides, it wasn't so comfortable to lay on clods of earth. I gathered the remained food, which was quite a lot, and put it back in the bag carefully. 'The pigs will love the polenta, and we could cook the cheese the way mother taught me. I cannot wait to go back home and do it, I love cooking!' I thought with excitement, then I stood up, folded the rug and put the bag on the soil, covering it with our jumpers. The water was finished, and I realised we didn't go to bring a fresh one.

"Papa, we forgot the water. Do you want me to go and bring some?"

"Are you thirsty?" he asked. "'Cause if you aren't, there is no point, it will get warm in a few minutes. I'll go when we need it."

'It makes sense,' I thought and started working in silence.

One hour later we heard someone calling my father's name. "Giuseppeee. I am here. I hope you've finished as I am in a terrible hurry."

I raised my head and saw Uncle John waving at us. 'Omg, he's early and we haven't finished!' But as soon as I thought that, I noticed that there were just a few beetroots left. 'Thank God!'

My father took the bag from the ground and asked me to finish while he went to help my uncle to put the beetroots inside the cart. "Hurry up and when you've finished, come to give us a hand."

I didn't reply just focused on the job. A few minutes later, the crop was completely empty. No beetroots were left in the soil. 'Hurray!' I exulted in my mind and started running towards my father and uncle. I reached them breathing heavily. "You see, Papa, we've finished. I told you we will, but you didn't want to believe it. You are no man of faith."

Both ignored my presence, so I moved my attention towards the beautiful horse who was eating some hay my uncle gave to him. That horse was huge, and I was terrified. I've always been fearful of big animals, cows, horses, bulls, pigs. Sometimes I was afraid of the roosters too, for good reasons though! They were very aggressive! Fifteen minutes later, all beetroots were gone. The cart waggon was almost full and Uncle John tide up the beautiful brown horse to it. I grabbed all the things we had and thrown them on top of the beetroots. My uncle commanded the horse to start going. The beetroots weight a lot and were thousands of them in that cart. The horse had to gather all his forces to make the cart moving.

The roads in the fields were heavily trafficked, several carts were passing by in both directions. Some were full of corn, beetroots, or potatoes; others were empty coming from the village, ready to be filled with different harvests. My heart was heavy and I thought of how much I disliked that season. I couldn't stand the way the animals were treated. We didn't have a horse or a cow because my father wasn't home to take care of them and us, children, were not very fond of animal exploitation in general.

There weren't many trucks or cars back then, horses or cows were used to bring home the entire production, and not only. We walked behind the cart for one kilometre or so, until the road became more secure. My uncle jumped on the cart, my father followed asking me to do the same.

"I'll walk, Papa."

"You cannot walk for ten kilometres again. It will take you more than 2 hours. It's getting dark, we need to take the beetroot to the collective and be home before 5 pm."

"No, I won't do it. I can't. The cart is too heavy. That poor horse will die."

"Don't be silly," intervened Uncle John, "it's nothing for him. You aren't fat, jump on already, or I'll leave you here in the middle of nowhere alone."

I didn't like to be left alone in the dark, ten kilometres away from the village on a Saturday evening. I had no choice than to get on top of the beetroots, in the cart. I kept my breath, opened my arms, and grabbed on the two sides of the cart to be able to hold my body suspended. In my child mind, I thought and hoped that my body weight will have no impact on the horse. The beautiful animal didn't seem to notice, and it started galloping with ease. We reached the outskirts of the village in less than ten or fifteen minutes. From there we had other three kilometres till home. The cart slowed down, and I jumped off it fast.

"Cristinuza don't ever do that again. You could have hurt yourself. Next time wait for the horse to stop first. Besides, you should have stayed on."

"No, I will never, ever jump on a cart again. I thought I'll die. You have no idea how difficult that was. I held my breath for almost the whole way here. You didn't notice as you were speaking with Uncle John. Look at the cart, compare the weight of it with the weight of the horse. Does that seem fair to you? The cart is at least five times heavier than the animal! I cannot believe he could drag it all the way here. And with us on it!"

"Silly child, you are like a feather! It makes no difference for an animal! How will you survive in here?" Said my father with a sigh.

"Leave me alone, I am upset with both of you insensitive people."

We were at the *Collective* (the name gave to the association that took by force all the land from people) silos and left half of the cart to them—for the state. The other half was our part. That was the agreement. At first, we were supposed to take all these beetroots home because we've already given all the harvest from different pieces of land we finished two weeks before. But when the bosses realised they were not reaching the amount of the production required by the state decided to ask for more from those who had more land, and we needed to obey. To be honest, I was happy that the horse didn't have to carry all those beetroots into the village.

We left the *Collective* surroundings to go home. My father and uncle jumped into the cart, I refused categorically and started running behind it. I didn't like running, but it was the sacrifice I chose to make for the horse. At some point, the cart slowed down. I looked in front of me to understand why. There was a big hill a few metres ahead. I put a hand on my heart as to contain the pain that suddenly overwhelmed it. I rushed to reach my uncle who jumped off the cart too and was close to the horse. I knew what was coming. I witnessed this scene several times before. The animal was about to feel pain. I couldn't allow it this time.

As soon as my uncle raised his hand to hit the animal with a whip, I shouted, "Please, don't beat him, it hurts. I beg you."

Uncle John looked at me in disbelief, "What the..." and yelled to my father with rage, "Giuseppe, take your daughter from my sight immediately, or I swear to God I'll use this whip on her."

My father didn't expect that and wasn't prepared, but grabbed my hand to pull me aside. He never hit me and got very upset with my uncle for threatening me. "Don't you dare to hurt this soul! She's just a child, she doesn't know what life is yet. Don't mind her."

"What were you thinking? You know how Uncle John is, he could have hurt you!"

While my father was lecturing me, I heard the sound of the whip hitting the poor animal who made a terrible jump upfront from pain. I closed my eyes for a second to hold back my tears. I felt the power of the strike on my back, and I shouted as loud as I could, "Stop, please, STOOOP, you are hurting him."

My father grabbed my hand again and forced me to walk with him on the other side of the cart, away from my uncle who was saying to my father in disgust, "You have a very weird child, Giuseppe, not that the others were different. I have never seen anything like that. I pity you."

My father ignored him and tried to reason with me, "Cristinuza, this is madness. He's just an animal. They don't have souls."

I was sobbing in despair, "Who told you they don't have souls? But what does it matter? He's made of flesh and bones just like us! When someone hits you, you feel pain. It's the same for them. It hurts, Papa, it hurts. The body suffers, not the soul. You know that."

I was pushing the cart with all the forces I had, my father came close to me and start doing the same. "Cristinuza, he's just an animal. He was born for this."

"No, he was not! We don't have to hurt him! He's got a heart, you know. And it hurts when we hit him like it hurts when we get wounded. Why don't you understand this? Look at him, he's exhausted!"

"But how are we supposed to bring the harvest home then? We need to eat in order to survive."

"In that case, I won't eat anymore. I don't want to survive in a world like this. I don't like Autumns mostly because of this. We exploit animals, we hit them and they have no guilt. They haven't done anything wrong. Why are humans so merciless!" Thousands of tears were falling down my red cheeks. I was inconsolable.

"You'll see when you'll get older, you'll understand then. It's how things go. We have to adapt. Besides, we work as hard as he does."

"Maybe, but nobody hits us."

"Not nowadays... but it was like that for humans

too."

I looked at my father, of course he was right. I knew he was, but I was suffering for and with the poor animal who was breathing heavily. You could see how hard he tried. My father was sweating, I was sweating and... next to me it was Uncle John all red and tired. He was pushing too. The hill was over, we've stopped for a few minutes to gather our breaths, then we've started moving again.

I ran behind the cart, it wasn't long until home. We got there when it was already dark. The lights were on... Not the bulbs, the candles. The communists cut the electricity, of course. As every day for years now. I ran to search for my mother; she was weaving. "Mum, how are you feeling? Are you better now?"

"Yes. Where is your father?"

"He's outside, he's emptying the cart. They send me away, are upset with me."

"Why? What have you done?"

"Nothing..." I didn't want to say anything to her as she'd tell me exactly what my father explained before. They knew better, of course.

I went outside. Uncle John was gone, and my father went to check on the crop behind the house. I knelt on the ground, several tears were flowing down my red cheeks. I turned to God, "He will finally eat and rest now. Poor animal! Why did you do that? Why beings have to suffer?! I don't understand. It's above my capacities... You're mean, very mean. You make me cry. I don't like you anymore."

Suddenly, the outside light bulb illuminated. 'The electricity is back! Thank God. We could watch Jack Cousteau and the wonders of the sea life this evening. We all need some sort of entertainment.'

Then I went into the kitchen outside to look for hot water. I needed a bath. The door was closed, and it was very warm inside. In the stove were some shy flickering logs. I stopped and looked at the dancing shadows of the flames on the walls. I couldn't take my eyes off, it was mesmerising. I just loved the atmosphere in it. I didn't feel cold anymore. On the black metal hob was a huge silver cauldron full of hot water. The thick steam coming out of it was very reassuring. I felt grateful. I really needed a bath. I moved my eyes around the room scarcely illuminated by a candle, there wasn't electricity inside it, to find the bathtub. I spotted it on the floor, big, clean and grey. That meant all my siblings, and my mother too had a bath before, then cleaned it and left there ready for us.

We didn't have a bathroom in the house, we didn't have running water so no proper bathtub. The warmest room, like this kitchen now, was used as the bathroom. The bathtub, made from some sort of grey metal, was bought from my parents years ago. We all loved to have baths as often as possible. It was very important for us. We paid loads of money on it, and it was the biggest I've seen in my life. Very heavy and difficult to manage.

I took the hot water from the cauldron and poured it into the big bathtub. It was too hot so I had to add two buckets of cold water. I filled up the cauldron again so my father will be able to have a bath too. He was addictive to baths, even more than us.

I went in the house to bring a towel and clean clothes. It was night time, so the pyjamas were appropriate. My siblings were watching the TV.

I locked the door, covered the windows with thick

white curtains to have some privacy, and immersed my whole body in the bathtub. There were no shower creams or gels back then, so no bubbles. We had hard soaps made by my mother. They didn't smell nice, but were cleaning our skin well. I stayed in it for ten minutes dreaming about a hot shower in a proper bathroom. One of my sweetest dreams back then. Suddenly, I heard someone knocking on the door.

"Cristinuza, how long is it going to take? Do you need some help emptying the bathtub? I am outside if you need me." It was my father.

"Give me five minutes, Papa, I'm almost done. No need to help me, I'll manage, just bring the buckets in front of the door, please."

My father walked away. I came out of the bathtub, patched my body dry and dressed as quickly as possible. I didn't want my father to wait, it was late and he loved the documentary with Cousteau. He was his hero.

I went outside to find the buckets and using a big iron mug I emptied the bathtub and cleaned it for my father. I was about to go on the street to throw the water when my father came in and took both buckets from my hands telling me as usual, "It is chilly outside, you'll get a cold because your hair is still wet. You go in the house with the others and cover yourself with a blanket."

"But Papa..." I tried to argue.

"No but, do as I say."

I allowed my father to take the buckets on the street and I went inside the house, where my other family was watching TV. The light wasn't on, just the TV. Nobody moved when I got in, they didn't even notice.

My mother was alone in the back room, weaving. I went to ask how things were going.

"How long until you finish this rug, Mum?"

"I finished the rug last week, but I need to do one metre on the new one, so I could take it off. Your father is going tomorrow morning to sell it in the market."

"Do you need some help? Do you have enough wool?"

"Yes, go and sit with your siblings. I'll join you in a minute. Has your father had a bath yet?"

"He's in now," I replied and left to watch some TV in the other room.

My father joined us twenty-five minutes later. My mother came a little later. I could hear her cutting the rug and sewing the margins.

Around 10:30 pm, we switched off the television as the programmes were over. Yawning, we all took turns to the toilet outside. Then we went to sleep in different rooms, but at least two of us were sharing the same bed. I was sleeping with my mother in that period, that's because I was the second youngest. My little brother was sleeping with my father.

That evening, as every evening for eleven years, I prayed for that poor horse and for every being in the Universe, hoping nobody would suffer the next day. I heard my parents praying too. But I couldn't tell for what. I realised I didn't eat that evening, neither my father. We both forgot. And the food was on the table. 'What a waste. Other people would give anything to have that food.' I thought with sorrow and fell asleep with tears on my cheeks and prayers on my lips.

I remember this story as it was yesterday, every

time I see a dead copper leaf on the street. Autumns make me feel melancholic, and I wish for this season to never come. It is too gloomy. All the emotions experienced that day overwhelm me over and over again. I shed countless tears, ask for forgiveness and pray for that horse again, but not only. He is long gone now, same as my uncle. My father doesn't remember. He doesn't remember much from the previous day... If you'd ask my siblings, they will say nothing. It was a regular Autumn day for them. I was different. Everything was very intense for me since I was born. I lived with passion moments of happiness and sadness, and I remember a lot—too much—from my communist childhood.

I remember observing my siblings when they were doing and saying things. Trying to understand what they like and why.

I remember crying with my mother when she was extremely upset. I wished so much to take her pain away.

I still have a great recollection of the mud, the cold wind and how much I wanted to have a hot shower every day.

I recall the start of every scholastic year during the communists when they used to send village students in the fields instead of making them study Maths or read as the children from cities. All the discriminations, duties, rules, and exploitations; the shortage of fruits, toys, sweets and almost every vital aliment, the indigence... none of these will ever leave my memory.

But mostly, I remember how I felt when reading *Les Miserables.*

Father Frost and oranges

Christmas wasn't celebrated officially in my country during the communist regime.

Why? Because Christmas is about religion and God, and our ex-President didn't like competition.

Some say that Ceausescu was an atheist. It would make sense because he never spoke about God, went to a church, or was seen with a priest. No religion was ever mentioned in media (television, radio, or written paper). Our ex-president was famous for having razed to the ground several churches in the capital, but not only. So, yes, he could have been an atheist or a fervid fighter against God. I don't know.

If there was no Christmas, then there was no Santa Claus either, we would think. However, there was a Santa coming into town but was called differently. Not because my mother tongue is not English, but because it had a different name in my language too. I wouldn't know how to translate it exactly, but it is close to *Father Frost*. He came to visit children in schools and kindergartens, dressed as Santa Claus, but his name in public was *Father Frost*. At home, we called him with the real name.

Curious how I have never asked about this inconsistency. Again, I thought it was normal everywhere.

In schools, he brought us notebooks, pens and crayons and a candy maybe. All in a plastic bag, no fancy gift papers, and we were in ecstasy anyway, at least I was. I used to run home and show my mother the bag. I remember how I always took the candy from it, hid it in my little fist and fearful handing it to her while she was weaving.

"What are you having there?" she would always ask.

"Take it and, you'll find out. It's from Father Frost."

She would then stop weaving for a second, open one of her hands to allow me to drop whatever I had in my tiny fist. "A candy? How many did you have in the bag?"

"Just one," I would answer smiling.

"Then why are you giving it to me? Here, have it back. It's yours."

"No, I saved it for you. I don't like candies much."

It was true. I was never fond of candies, although some were absolutely delicious in that period. They don't make anything like that nowadays.

Why would a candy mean so much to me so I would write about it?

Because candies, sweets in general, were not vital for surviving so they were extremely difficult to find. Like toys, clothes, shoes, fruits, and everything you can think of. I said this before.

Our country was going through an extreme period of indigence, and not because it was poor, but because the President decided to impose all sorts of shortages to pay the debts he made without thinking. Therefore, electricity was given for a few hours a day, mostly very early in the morning, so the women were forced to wake up at 4 am to bake bread.

The same happened with the running water. Timetables. We were not affected by that because we had no plumbing in the house. Only people living in the cities in communist blocks would pay that price.

Chocolate, exotic fruits, cookies, or sweets were sold underhand to friends and family. Same as meat, sausages, salami, any type of food made from meat was a real treat for many. You know this already.

Toys were even more difficult to find and I didn't see many in my childhood. I had no idea they existed, to be honest, and I didn't miss them. The Regime considered these a frivolity, not vital for surviving. All you could find in shops was made in my country, and the quality was outstanding. Unfortunately, for the people born in villages was extremely rare to see any toy whatsoever in the local shops.

My mother's told me that she heard stories of people buying toys from our shop, but she never managed to put her hands on to any because she wasn't a friend of any retailer.

Yes, you had to be friends or family or bribe the retailer to have a toy or something that wasn't easy to find.

Corruption was absolutely normal back them. Anyone could have been bribed. Teachers to give better votes and higher or false prizes. Retailers to sell you underhand all sorts of things. Bartenders for a better glass of vodka. Team leaders to allow you to stay home. Doctors to give you a shot or a certificate. Drivers to let you get on the bus. Office workers for any document. Every single person who had power over something was open to a potential bribery. At any time, for any reason. Yes, that was how things were going in my country.

That's why I never got a better prize in school, although I was one of the best students. I used to come home every single day with A+. My parents were surprised to see I didn't get the crown, but they were rules-followers, "never question who's got more power than you." They felt inferior because they didn't have diplomas, but I can assure you that my parents were smarter than most people I knew back then. I cared about reading, not the crowns, but maybe I should have. Too late now.

I didn't want toys, either because I wasn't an ordinary child, or because I was happy doing things around my parents. I used to spend most of my time watching my mother weaving, cooking, or doing the laundry (by hand), and my dad fixing the bicycle. I was mesmerised and didn't have time for anything else. Nevertheless, I had a doll in my life, and the day I saw her decapitated, it was one of the scariest of my life.

***

I was about five, I think. It was a regular Friday evening. The house was scarcely illuminated by some candles strategically placed in glasses filled with corn flour.

Why?

Well, weren't candles like the ones you see nowadays. They were very thin and forty centimetres or even one metre long. It depended on the use you'd make and the money you were prepared to pay for it. Votive candles. They emanated a reasonable amount of light, but also a black smoke accompanied by a terrible smell. These candles were white, and I liked that, moreover, they were useful when the communist regime stopped the electricity at regular intervals or without notice. Happened every day for whole my childhood.

That Friday night, I was in the house with my little brother, God knows what I was doing when an older sister got in. I haven't seen her for a few weeks as she was studying at a boarding school most of the year. I went to hug her, then she went to speak with my parents and other siblings. They were discussing something, but I didn't pay attention. I was happy to see my sister after such a long time. Fifteen minutes later she came to me and asks me to look out of the door window, into the corridor. It was dark, as I said, but I could individuate a silhouette leaning against the wall. I turned around and asked what that was. She then said to look better or go and check in person. I was afraid, I didn't like dark much. I stayed inside the house looking out that small window for a few minutes until I realised that was a girl, a little taller than me, wearing a fabulous blue dress. I gained courage and went to see who was it, thinking it was one of my nieces. —Yes, I have nieces older than me as two of my elderly sister got married before I was born.—I opened the door and got face to face with this silhouette. It was a girl indeed, but it seemed not to move at all. I touched her hand a little, it was kinda cold. Very weird sensation. I looked carefully, and as I didn't recognise her, I turned over my sister to ask who was that again. The whole family was gathered around observing my every reaction.

"Cristina, it's a doll. Isn't she beautiful?" said my sister.

"A doll?! What does it mean?"

"A toy, you can play with it. It is yours only. You can comb her hair, look..." she explained while grabbing the doll in her arms. The body didn't move nor said anything and I realised with wonder that she was made of plastic.

"Omg," I shouted excited. "She is not a person? She looks like one. I love her hair!" I hold her tight in my arms for several minutes. But she was taller than me and it was an amusing scene to watch.

That was the very first time I saw a doll. I've seen others after that, but they didn't belong to me. My brunette doll was the biggest of them all, the most beautiful, she was just gorgeous.

I jumped around for hours and didn't want to go to sleep. I am not sure if my parents allowed me to bring her to bed with me, I have no recollection of me sleeping next to the doll. Ever. What I do remember is the Sunday in which my doll lost her head. Literally.

I was playing with some children, maybe neighbours, perhaps my nieces and nephews. I put the doll on a table, pretending she was ill and I was the doctor in charge of visiting her.

I turned around to take something, and the next thing I saw was the head of my doll rolling down the ground. All of a sudden, without anyone touching her. Her long black hair was all over her face. She looked hideous.

I screamed and cried in horror for hours. "My doll is dead, and I killed her! I am going to burn in hell forever."

My parents tried to explain to me that it wasn't me doing anything to her. "A doll cannot die and she could be easily fixed silly girl," said my father. My mother assured me that I was not going to burn in hell for that, maybe for other reasons, but definitely not for that. My siblings were laughing with tears, but when they realised I was really traumatised, they went to look for my older brother— who was a very resourceful young man—and told him the story. My older brother put her head back in a few minutes, but I refused to touch that toy again.

All my siblings were disappointed, but none could convince me that was normal and I shouldn't be scared. I asked them to give the fixed doll away because the view of her silhouette scared me to death. Therefore, the doll with blue eyes and long black hair was given to an older sister who had another one, same height just different outfit and haircut. Both were placed on a piece of antique furniture in my sister's house, but I have never asked to play or touch any of them again.

When I think of this story now, I recognise that the murmured discussion between my parents and my siblings was about the doll. They were debating if the doll should be given to me right away, or wait for Christmas. Because they were more excited than me, the grand majority won and let me have it right then. Santa Claus brought me something else that following Christmas.

I now know that my siblings were asked by my mother to buy toys for the youngest of us from the cities where they were studying.

That doll cost an awful amount of money, but no one remembers how much so I cannot tell.

After that unfortunate experience, my whole family decided I shouldn't have another doll again. They wrote a long letter to Santa, explaining the situation and asking him to bring me something else, anything, just not a doll. Believe it or not, Santa followed that unusual request. It wasn't that difficult in the end, there was a severe shortage of dolls in my country anyway.

As I already mentioned, Christmas was completely ignored publicly. At home, people knew that Jesus was born on the night of twenty-fourth of December and we all celebrated his birth in churches. We were free to do that because my village was very far away from the Capital, but after the fall of the communist regime, many people recounted that they were not allowed to go to churches. Believers in God were constrained to hide and gather in secret locations, usually houses that belonged to unsuspected people like leaders, teachers, doctors and so on. In there they had to keep their voices down, which meant that were no singing.

This reminded me of *Quo Vadis, A Narrative of the Time of Nero*, a historical novel about the Christianity and the tortures they were subjected to, written by Henryk Sienkiewicz.

Winter festivities was called the period from the 27th of December until the 2nd of January. And although schools would all close on the 22nd of December, Christmas was not officially included in this winter festivities.

Rigorously, on the 24th of December, families would decorate a fir tree with lights, shiny spheres, candies, and chocolate, but it was called *Winter tree*, not Christmas tree. This was kept inside. To the day, it's still in my country tradition to keep the Christmas tree inside the house, however, in the last years, people have started to adopt Western traditions like decorating any sort of tree they might have in front of the house.

The perfume of the evergreen tree was inebriating, especially if you had a stove or a fireplace with crackling fire in the house. It was the best period of the whole year. The snow, the preparations, the cooking, baking, gathering together in the same room.

I loved the snow immensely. The first snowing day of the year, if it happened during the night, which was very common, my mother would wake up earlier than usual and asked us to look out of the window. My little brother and I were so excited that we couldn't wait to get dressed to go outside, but we'll run out without shoes, in pyjamas and dance in the snow. Roll jump and get completely wet. Pure magic.

Christmas time was heaven on Earth for my family. We had everything we needed, parents, siblings, plenty of food, loads of home-baked cakes and cookies. The siblings who left, either because they got married or went to work in faraway cities, would come home and celebrate with us.

The temperatures were extremely low, sometimes got under 30 °C, so we would cover our bodies in several layers of warm clothing, made from wool mostly. We would all gather and sleep in two small rooms. That's because we couldn't afford to heat all the rooms we had and used during more amiable times of the year.

In these rooms were only three double beds. Clearly not enough for fifteen or twenty people. So we would put some heavy duvets, amazing work made by my mother, on the floor and the children would fight for those temporary beds. I absolutely loved sleeping on the floor under the Christmas tree. Unlike my father who always tried to persuade us, the little ones, to sleep in beds instead.

"Cristinuza, you could catch a cold, please, go and sleep with your mother, near your older sisters."

But I was very stubborn and never changed my decision of sleeping on the floor. It was the best thing that could happen to me in that period, after the snow.

The stoves would burn wood continuously and hearing or watching the crackling fire was utterly mesmerising. Every night I would fall asleep watching the shadows of the flames dancing on the walls. I was so happy that I was afraid my heart would explode from too much joy. I have never experienced a more perfect sensation than that.

The saddest part of this story is the fact that more than a half of the country didn't have the means to buy and decorate a tree—that was considered the richest people's right. Half of the population didn't have a lot of food to put on the table. For many, home-baked bread, cookies, and cakes were just impossible dreams.

My family wasn't rich, but we were farmers and worked every day of the year on the land or around the house. We raised countless animals and birds, so we had plenty of meat for the most part of the year. We prepared sausages, salami, and other delicatessen that many were only fantasising about. We grew several types of vegetables and trust me when I tell you that was demanding, extremely, but we loved it. We had no free days, except Sundays. We went to school as it was fundamental to our education and we never missed a day. We loved school very much. But we also enjoyed helping our parents with the farm. We've worked hard and that was why we always had plenty of food. We've never starved as you might have heard other people saying.

Anyway, let's get back to Christmas and Santa Claus or Father Frost.

It was magical for us for all the reasons enumerated in precedence, but also because at Christmas we always met Santa Claus in person. Every year I sat on his lap and told him a poem.

He didn't come when we were sleeping, put the gifts under the tree and eat the biscuits. No, he would shout "Ho, ho, ho," knock on the door and wait for us to say "come in," and when he got in, was a perfect fairy tale. Red and white costume, long hair, and white beard, carrying a big bag on his shoulders full of presents for all of us. Body curved, trembling hands covered in gloves.

The youngest would shake from fear and emotion. Santa always knew everything about each of us and sometimes we didn't behave, so it was both a happy moment, but also a terrifying one. So many mixed feelings and so many tears shed.

The first recollection of him it's from when I was two. He brought me a red telephone. Not just any telephone, but the one I told my mother about. An antique one. A toy, of course. When I opened the pack, I couldn't believe my eyes. I shouted and jumped on my feet like a happy goat and run to show it to my mother, who would always sit close to the stove when Santa was there.

"Mum, look, it's exactly what I wanted! Remember when I told you about it a few months back? How did he know?"

"Santa knows everything, baby girl," my mother said.

It might be difficult to believe that I could actually have such a vivid memory from a very young age, but it is true. The image of the phone, the one I dreamt about, had a remarkable impact on my whole existence. The physical presence of Santa in our house, the tree, and the whole family reunited made me feel emotions impossible to describe in words. It was pure paradise.

I drove my mother crazy with that telephone. I played with it every day for countless hours. I made it rang continuously, forming random numbers and talking with imaginary people. My mother begged me to stop many times, but I never did. It got broken in a few months from too much use. My father tried to fix it, but I lost a piece of it and didn't ring anymore.

If you think that my mother managed to still a fundamental piece of it, you have to think twice and here is why.

It was around September, the following year when my mother asked me what I will make my sister write the letter to Santa.

"What do you want for Christmas, the baby girl?"

"I want a telephone. Exactly like the one I had last year. Red."

"Are you sure you don't want a dress or a pair of shoes maybe?" my mother tried to reason with me.

"No, I want the red telephone or nothing."

Santa brought me *The Telephone,* of course. I was in tears as I really didn't think he will bring me the same gift two years consecutively. I was utterly amazed and couldn't stay in my skin from happiness. My mother could have asked Santa to bring me something else but she didn't want to disappoint her youngest daughter.

As I said, Santa was old, trembling from all his muscles.

"Why does he have such a long white beard and hair, Mum? And why is he wearing a mask?!" I asked every year after Santa's left.

My mother would then sit on the bed, took my little brother and me close, and told us the story of Santa Claus, "Santa was born many, many years ago in a very faraway continent. He is extremely old and that's why he's got such long and white hair. As for the mask, one year his sleigh broke down just when he was about to leave his house to come and bring gifts to all children of the world. He didn't have time to fix it, it was very late already, so he decided to take an aeroplane. Unfortunately, when he was going back, the plane crashed and got on fire. He managed to survive, but all his body and especially his face is full of terrible scars. He is hideously disfigured and wears the mask to not scare the children."

We were horrified to hear the story and were listening in silence. It all made sense, of course.

"But why are his hands and voice always shaking and covered in gloves?" I would ask again.

"Because he is timeworn and weak and because his hands are full of burned cicatrices. They don't look nice. You know what your cousin's arm looks like because he got burned, right?"

We both nodded "Yes" in fear, and my mother continued, "That's why whole his body has to be covered. He is also always in pain."

"But if he is so old and his body so ugly, why doesn't he ask someone else to bring children gifts?"

"He was born for this. His life would have no purpose if he wasn't Santa Claus."

"Does he have someone to help him preparing all these presents?"

"Of course. He's got many small people working for him."

We were utterly fascinated, shocked by the story and felt extremely sorry for Santa. We admired his will to continue bringing joy to the children of the entire world, despite being so old and tired.

***

Another Christmas Eve, when I was four maybe, I was playing with my little brother when we heard a knock on the door. We've stopped playing and looked around the house for our older siblings. They were nowhere to be found. We've looked one at another as to ask, "what should we do?" when my mother shouted from the other room,

"Go and check who's at the door, children. Didn't you hear someone knocking?"

We didn't even know she was in the other room. We thought we were left alone, but because we were so focused on playing, we didn't notice.

Although the clock showed 6 pm it was completely dark outside. The house was illuminated only by the Christmas tree lights. I was afraid, I didn't know who was at the door, but I was the oldest, so I gathered all my courage and went to look out the window. In front of the door was a man with long hair and white beard. I couldn't see the clothes he was wearing. I started shouting that outside was a very scary old man and I ran away from the door. My poor little brother hid under the bed terrified.

My mother then said, "Maybe it's Santa Claus!"

Of course we were very eager to see Santa Claus but didn't expect him to get to our house at that hour.

"So early!?" I asked surprised.

"Well, he has billions of children to visit tonight,

he must have stopped here first. Go and open the door, don't keep him waiting too long as he might think there is no one home, so he will leave to the next house."

This discussion took only a few seconds and when I heard that he might leave, I jumped and ran to open the door wondering where the heck were my other siblings!

"Ho, ho, ho," said Santa with a very trembling voice. "I almost left as I thought this house is deserted. Other children are waiting."

He called me by name, and that was madness. Then he told me that I was a good child and deserved a great present. "But I will only give it to you after you've recited the last poem you learned in kindergarten. You did learn one, right? I heard you drove your mother crazy with it."

Of course I learned one, but I couldn't get my head around about how could he possibly know all that about my other siblings and me. While I was reciting loud and clear, sitting on Santa's lap, my other siblings got in. I didn't stop, but it was very curious that behaviour.

I finished the poem, Santa gave me a big pack, then he asked my little brother for a poem, but he was too afraid to speak and Santa was very disappointed. He almost refused to give the present to my little brother in tears. In the end, he gave it to him and shared other small presents to all those in the house. Even my mother got one. She opened it to find some orange balls.

"What are these, Mum?" I curiously asked. "Balls? But you don't play with balls! You can give them to Sebi," (my little brother).

My mother burst into tears and I couldn't understand why.

"Forgive me," I said feeling extremely guilty for making my mother cry. "You don't have to give them to Sebi. You can keep them for you if you like. Sebi's got his present." I was crying too. I could never witness at someone crying without doing that myself.

But my mother took a ball and started peeling it. As soon as she peeled a small piece of that orange ball, the house filled with the most divine perfume I ever smelled. The ball looked naked without the orange skin. When my mother divided it into slices, loads of juice fell on the floor. One of my brothers brought a plate and asked my mother to do that operation above it so nothing would go to waste. When that was done, my mother took the first slice and gave it to my little brother. Then she took another one and gave it to me and so on. In five minutes every member of the family had a slice of orange in their hands.

"Eat it, it's a fruit called orange. Very delicious." She was right, it was more than delicious. The delicate slightly sour taste made me fall irremediably in love with that exotic fruit which looked like a perfect ball.

I've never seen an orange before, maybe only on television, but as it was the black and white era, I didn't know they were in fact orange! There were many things we didn't see or imagined during the communist regime. We only knew how to work the land, follow the rules without questioning, and praise the leaders of the country.

My mother was crying from emotion. She saw oranges before, but she never tasted one. She loved them! It was love at first sight for me. I am not sure my little brother felt the same.

My other siblings must have seen those fruits before, I never asked, but I am guessing they were the ones buying those oranges. Most certainly, one of my older sisters brought them from very far away for my mother. She was known for doing wonderful surprises.

*

Every time I peel an orange, that memory comes back exactly as that evening when I was overwhelmed by pain from seeing my mother crying, and by happiness when understanding why she reacted so.

Oranges were my mother's favourite fruits during the Communism, and we always did the impossible to bring some to her every time we could. But they were nowhere to be found during the year, only in the winter, when the winter festivities got closer. My siblings who were studying or working in distant cities would go every day to look for them. They used to stay in queues for several hours in extremely harsh temperatures to buy a few at once.

Because the scarcity of these magical fruits, the retailers would only sell one kilogramme to each person. As we were a large family, one kilogramme was never enough. My siblings tried to explain a few times why they needed more, but nobody listened.

"Either you are buying one kilogramme, or nothing," was always their reply.

Some other times they were just sold two oranges at once, so they will go and sit in line in a different shop and the next day again, dressed in a different way to not be recognised.

***

A regular day of October, I came home from

kindergarten and went to my room to get changed from the communist uniform. My little brother remained to play with some friends in front of the house. On the bed, there was a very colourful wide box. 'What is this and why it's on my bed?' I wondered. I took it and opened it with care. Inside were several plastic figurines, soldiers exactly. I had a look at the box, but I couldn't read so I didn't understand a word. It was obvious though that it was a battle game. A strategic one and I fell in love with the idea of playing it. I rushed inside the house to search for my mother who was weaving in the other room.

"Mum, muuuuum. What's that box on my bed?"

My mother blanked and quietly said, "I don't know. Go ask your older siblings."

I ran and called out aloud the names of all my siblings I knew were home. I could barely breathe from excitement. I found them working in the garden.

"What's that box with the soldiers on my bed?"

My siblings looked one at another, and one spoke up, "It's a gift for a neighbour of ours." A name I knew was revealed. "Their parents came to us and asked if we could keep it safe, so the child won't find it before his birthday. You know how curious he is. He will find it, no matter where his parents would hide it in the house. Please, don't say anything to anyone."

"I love it! I wish Santa will bring me one just like that."

"But that's a boy's game!" one of my siblings said.

"I don't care."

What do you think Santa brought me that

year?! The strategic game, of course! I couldn't stay in my skin from happiness and surprise.

"How did he know, Mum? How does he always know what I want? Is he God?"

"Very close, baby girl, very close."

***

But Santa didn't visit us every year. When I was seven, he didn't come. My little brother and I were broken-hearted. My older siblings were terribly sad for us. We refused to have dinner and were sitting around the table with the eyes inundated by tears. "Have we upset Santa that much?" I asked in a low voice.

"No, silly," replied one of our older sisters, "he might be too busy, or he lost track of time. The world is huge, you know. And you are not the only children in it. Maybe he will just leave something under the tree this year. As he does for all other children in the village."

"But we want to see him," I said unhappily.

My siblings tried to cheer us up, with little success. We were utterly devastated, and the atmosphere in the house wasn't festive at all. Both my parents were away that evening. Curious thing. One of my older sisters went out for a few minutes. She came back all feverish. "Look what I found! It must have been Santa leaving them outside the door," she said while handing us some gifts very well wrapped.

"But why didn't he come in and how come we didn't hear him?" asked my little brother not at all content having the gifts and no Santa.

Our brothers and sisters didn't have an answer for us. There were looking one at another completely lost. My sister then took Peter, a nine-year-old-brother of mine, by hand and both went out. Five minutes later she came back without my brother.

"I sent Peter to look for Santa. Maybe he's missed the house or God knows what happened."

We were swinging absent in our chairs when the door was slammed against the wall with power. Peter got in all agitated, carrying loads of candies in his arms. "Santa, Santa, I saw Santa! I swear! He's stopped his sleigh for a second and left these for you," shouted my brother while giving us the candies. "He said he's sorry for not being able to come in to say hello, but he's busiest than other years. He also said that he's left some other gifts for you before, and he hopes you like them."

As soon as we heard the word *Santa*, my little brother and I jumped to our feet feeling very emotional.

"Where was he? Maybe we could still see his sleigh. We've never seen it. What about the reindeer?" I asked excited.

Peter looked a little confused and my sister stepped in, "Yes, maybe we could watch him flying in the sky. Quick, let's all go outside! Where did you see him, Peter? Show us."

"In the street, in front of the house." Peter ran to point us the exact place.

All my siblings followed him. Sebi and I were trembling like leaves in the wind. We had no shoes on and were wearing pyjamas, but that wasn't the reason we were shaking, we were electrified by emotion. The noise the snow made when my siblings stepped on it, is unforgettable. We all looked carefully on the ground. It was very dark, but we could actually see some traces on the snow. "Here," I said to my little brother. "Look, Sebi, he's lost some candies." I bent to grab a few. "So it is true, he's been here indeed. He didn't forget us, Sebi, he didn't!!!"

We both checked the sky meticulously, but we couldn't catch a glimpse of his sleigh anywhere. Peter pointed to a very faraway light and said, "I think he is leaving the country now. Can you see that light looking like a star? It's him, I am sure of it."

My sister took my little brother in her arms and guided his eyes in the same direction, "Do you see that Sebi? It means Santa was here for real."

Our moods changed completely. The smile came back on all our eyes and faces. We stand there contemplating the street, it was deserted. Some houses had the Christmas tree lights on, others were completely submersed in the dark. But I will never forget how peaceful and serene everything looked. We gazed inside our house through the window, and it appeared magical as always, but we didn't notice it before because we were focused on Santa.

We went inside, leant against the stove to dry our clothes and we talked about Santa for a few hours. Everybody had a story about him. We laughed, giggled and ate oranges. My parents were still not back. I wondered if my mother will cry again at the view of the oranges.

We went to sleep feeling blessed and woke up with the smell of delicious food prepared by my mother. The house was warm and peaceful. We had no carols to listen to. There was no programme on television. I didn't make a sound and watched my mother moving quietly around the house. I used to do that very often when nobody looked. I watched my siblings and my father too. It was my secret. I loved observing people and animals trying to understand why we do what we do, what makes us happy or unhappy, what we like and dislike. The differences puzzled and fascinated me.

My mother caught me staring at her, she came close and said in a very low voice, "Look outside. It has been snowing for hours. There is another metre of snow on the streets. Your father makes channels in the courtyard so you could go and play with your brother later."

"Mum, where were you last night?"

"Shh... your siblings are still asleep and you should too. It's holiday."

On the table were some oranges and the peel of one was put in a bottle of water. My mother thought of surprising us and make us try some water with orange taste. I felt immensely blessed, and I prayed for those who had no mother to cook for them, no siblings to go and look for Santa, no father to clean the snow, no Christmas tree and no special dishes or cookies on that day.

***

When I was eight, Santa brought me a fabulous blue dress with many frills. I loved it very much and spend hours admiring it.

I sat on his lap no more, but I recited a long poem that one of my sister's taught me—*The death of the deer* by Nicolae Labis (a great Romanian poet who died in an accident at twenty-one—allegations involving *The Securitate* still travel around). I heard Santa snivel, but of course, we couldn't see his face. He caressed my hair and congratulated me for being of such great help to my mother. I couldn't believe he knew that too.

***

When I was nine and my little brother seven and a half, Santa didn't show up once again. All siblings went to look for him, but there was no trace of him anywhere. It was raining instead of snowing. They couldn't stay long outside as it was very cold. We waited for hours melancholically and finally went to bed very disappointed. My brother and I sobbed for hours. One of my sisters gave us oranges and bananas, but we didn't want anything. I didn't like bananas, and my little brother refused to even look at them. My parents went to visit some familiars. We went to bed utterly devastated.

It was one or two o'clock when we got woke up by our siblings shouting that Santa was there. We opened the eyes, but we couldn't see much. Our siblings kept saying it was Santa and he would like to say *hello*.

My little brother started crying. He didn't like to be awakened and yelled at in the middle of the night. He looked at Santa very carefully and his crying intensified, "He is not Santa, he is Peter!!! Cristina, he is Peter I am telling you."

I didn't want to believe and I argued, "Why would Peter wear Santa's clothes?"

"Because there is no Santa! My colleagues told me, but I saw Santa every year, and I thought they were lying because they never met Santa. He never went to their houses, but he always came to ours!"

"How can you say there is no Santa if last year he brought me a blue dress and oranges to mum?"

"It was our father! Santa is just a fairy tale."

"What?!"

The whole sky fell over my head. It seemed the end of the world. I was in such a shock! I looked at my siblings and at Santa who took the mask off defeated. It was true, Peter was dressed as Santa.

"How...?!" I murmured heartbroken.

My siblings avoided to look into my eyes. None had the courage to speak.

"Santa is one of us? A myth? That is why Papa was never present when Santa was here? Why didn't I ask myself this before? How did you manage to keep this secret for all these years? Does mum know? Of course she does. She once missed from home... that year when Santa..., Father didn't show up... She went to look for him, didn't she?! And you too Peter went to look for him. But nobody found him. Why, where was he?" I asked all these questions out loud. "Where was he that night? And where was he tonight?!?" Nobody spoke and I shouted, "Where is he now?"

"He went to give presents to other children in the village. He is the Santa to the whole place, not only to us," said one of my sisters in a very low voice.

"What? How could he go and do that for other children, but not for us?!"

"It's because you both are older now and those children are very young. You can wait longer than little children. Our parents and we planned this very well, but this evening is heavily raining, and he went on the other side of the village, you know how far away is that. It takes more than one hour to get here. He couldn't get back in time because he had many other very young children to visit. It got extremely late and nobody can walk on a night like this. The streets are skating rinks—very dangerous. We don't know anything about them and are worried sick. We pray that they are fine and maybe decided to sleep somewhere else."

I started to worry too. My little brother stopped sobbing and looked at me scared. He was afraid for my parents. I tried to look back with a very reassuring gaze, but he became more and more frightened. He loved my parents immensely.

"That night he didn't show up again, was because he slipped on the ice and hurt himself very badly. My mother went to look for him that night and this one too. They are still in the village. But we have no idea of where to look for them. We went to a few places, but they left and didn't manage to meet," explained with sadness one of my sisters.

We waited for a few hours but fell asleep eventually.

When we got up the Christmas day, my mother was cooking and my father was sleeping. We forgot about Santa Claus, the gifts, and the sleigh. We were grateful to see them both home. We were also sorry for my brother who did his best to keep the myth alive.

My eyes opened that year and my heart filled with the most profound love for all my family. I now know why my father was never present when Santa was in our house. Why were my older siblings and my mother always away before the arrival of Santa; I know who bought the gifts and from where; who helped my father to get ready. I know how difficult was to do all those things and not be discovered. If in the late years, my older siblings were the ones in charge to look for the perfect gifts for the youngest, before my time was only my mother the one who took care of that and she told me that she used to go twenty kilometres on foot to find these toys.

Why on foot? Because when it snowed a lot we

were cut off the world. She's told me that the snow was so high that every step she took, made her sank into the snow, so she had to stop and helped the leg to come out with her hands. It was tough and many people would have never done it. My mother did.

If you're asking yourself why did they wait until the last minute, well, they had no other choice. The toys were sold in the city shops two weeks before Christmas, and most of the time were already sold before seeing the shelves. Relatives, friends, friends of friends paid large amounts of money for specific toys. People like my mother, who didn't know any shop assistant, had to go from one shop to another, and pray God to find some toys, any toys for that matter.

I could never express enough gratitude to all my siblings and parents who did everything in their power and much more to make us feel children of the world, not slaves of Ceausescu, at least at Christmas. Those years were the best of my life, despite the hard conditions of life. But I knew that couldn't stay like that forever.

The 25th of December 1989–The end

From 1967 to 1989, Ceausescu decided who had the right to live and who had to die; how many children a woman should have; who was entitled to study, and who was doomed to work the land. We were not free to travel outside the country, we were not allowed to speak our minds, to protest or complain. He had all the imaginable and unimaginable power over our lives.

He didn't care you were a child, and all you wanted was to play with toys, no. If you were a farmer's child, you were required to help your parents and your school to reach the country's targets.

He kept us in the dark about the rest of the world, censored movies and songs, cut the power and the hot water for nineteen hours a day, rationalised food like we were living a war. He treated his people as slaves and expected them to endure all this forever with a smile on the faces.

In 1977 miners from Targu Jiu went on strike because of inhumanly conditions of work. The leader of the country ordered his army to shoot them dead—all of them. But the army didn't listen, and some changes had to be made for those poor miners.

Because these atrocities were never reached the mass media, we don't know how many of them took place. We heard rumours about thousands of killings, but we knew nothing for certain.

Every single person in the country was on their knees. We had no idea that the rest of the world had a different style of life, but we knew something was not quite right. We were hopeless.

There is a belief going around humans who didn't experience anything of the above. We think that if people don't know about the existence of something, they will always be happy with what they have. I completely agree with that. I am the first one to sustain this theory. However, we all wanted something we never saw on a daily basis.

We didn't have a fridge, washing machine, running water in the house, books, chocolate and so on. None of the people I knew had these either, but we watched some movies from time to time, and seeing how easier their life was, made us desire the same.

I didn't miss the chocolate, for example, because I never really liked it that much. But every Saturday, the day in which we used to have a *serious* bath, I dreamed and craved for a shower. I used to imagine myself having at least two showers a day, and that was one of my sweetest dreams. I fantasised about going to school for whole my life and read the books I wanted at the light of an electric bulb.

My little brother loved ice cream, same as my mother and most of my siblings, and if you'd asked him what would he buy if he had the means, he would have told you, "A freezer so I could fill it with ice cream."

My mother always dreamed about a proper colour television with a remote control.

One of my sisters was mad about coffee, another one about caviar.

All the children I ever knew wanted chewing gum—loads of colourful chewing stuff. If everywhere in the world chewing gum was one of the easiest things to find, I believe that in my country was prohibited back then. I am not sure, of course, but no shop ever sold this odd sweet. However, I have chewed it many times after my siblings went to school, 500 kilometres away. In these distant big cities, foreigners would bring and sell loads of illegal or impossible to find stuff like coffee, play cards, cigarettes, porn magazines and chewing gum. This last one was made in forms of cigarettes and put in colourful packs of twelve. These packs contained imagines of football or tennis-men players, gymnasts, athletes or singers. Some of them were Romanian, and we were absolutely crazy for both images and chewing gum.

Once, my uncle asked a group of children what would they want him to bring them the next time he visits. I was in that group, and all of us, absolutely all, replied in a choir, "chewing gum." My uncle was shocked and tried to persuade us to ask for other things like chocolate, clothes, or religious objects, but we were resolute, "Chewing gum, nothing else."

***

In December of 1989, several people from Timisoara protested against the arrest of a religious leader they cared for. Of course that was not shown on television or announced on the national radio station. We lived very far away from the Capital and Timisoara and didn't have any relatives in there to let us know about this. However, my father knew about an illegal radio station that transmitted from Germany—*Radio Free Europe*—which had an hour in Romanian, for Romanians. I don't recall if they broadcasted every evening, but I remember how terrified was my father that someone could find us listening to it. Therefore, one of us had to stay on guard outside the house for the whole broadcasting period. We couldn't tell anyone about it and trust no one. *The Securitate*—Romanian secret police—had infiltrated everywhere. Anyone could have been an agent: your wife, husband, child, brother, boss, friend, even or especially the priest.

Thousands of people were incarcerated and tortured every day based on allegations or rumours. The only person you could trust was God because he didn't speak.

The Timisoara event has been spread in the country by the *Radio Free Europe* and gave people a push to start a real protest in the Capital. People knew that Ceausescu was heartless, and their lives were at stake, but the austerity and the extreme conditions outrun the desire of being safe.

On the 21st of December 1989, when the leader who oppressed his country for over twenty-two years started to give one of his regular speeches in the *Palace Square*—now known as the *Revolution Square*—many people began booing and chanting, "Timisoara."

Ceausescu tried to control the crowd by raising his hands but after a few temporary tranquil moments, and when he said that the minimum wage will increase, people couldn't bear anymore. The square became a chaos, and the intensified booing scared the dictator who took cover into a building.

I saw those images hundreds of times, and I cannot get my head around of why he looked so shocked about it.

Of course he gave instructions to shoot all the rioters, but once again the army refused to follow his orders. Soldiers were heard saying, "It could be my brother in there, I won't kill my family. I can't." The Securitate then executed on sight several of these soldiers, but that didn't stop the crowd. In a matter of minutes, the population of Bucharest and other big cities were on the streets chanting, "Down with Ceausescu, Down with the Communist Party."

Ceausescu wanted to run and hide, maybe outside the country, but he was not prepared for that eventuality. I guess he was convinced that the country loved him and an insurrection was never a possibility.

He was caught along with his wife and on the 25th of December—Christmas day—before a kangaroo court, both were accused of many things, but what I remember was genocide and illegal gathering of wealth. Of course they denied all the accusations and refused to answer any questions repeating over and over again that they would only answer in front of the *Big National Assembly*.

Nevertheless, they were found guilty and sentenced to death which took place on the same day.

The trial and shooting were broadcasted in the whole country, maybe the whole world, I really don't know. We switched the television on outside the regular hours of airing because of the revolution and because Ceausescu's lost power over everything. My family and I were gathered in the living room. Our hearts were filled with mixed emotions, the sense of liberation and the sorrow for those people.

During the whole broadcasting period, we cried and prayed for the souls of the people who enslaved us for over twenty-two years. Personally, I couldn't watch that show. It seemed unreal and not right.

That year we forgot about oranges, Santa Claus or Father Frost, gifts, and celebrations. For us, that

Christmas didn't symbolise the birth of Jesus, but the death of two people who had nothing human inside them. But we suffered anyway. I couldn't imagine myself in the same situation, it was too painful. That night we went to bed with a new burden on our shoulders.

***

Nowadays if you'd go and ask Romanians over the age of thirty-five about Ceausescu's era, most of them would say that we should have never killed them. They will assert that it was so much better during that period. More than 70% of the Romanian population wants Ceausescu back.

But I have my memories, like many other people, and I can assure you that Christmas day in December of 1989, all Romanians would have pulled the trigger. With no exception.

I am amazed of how people forget things like slavery, genocide, austerity, censures.

We were treated worse than animals, and we want him back?

It is true that my country is not doing well, but we have Freedom. We can travel and look for new opportunities if we want to. It is not easy, but it's simple.

My passport states I am Romanian, the truth is I am a citizen of the World.

If Communism hadn't fallen that year, God only knows what would have happened. We couldn't take it anymore. They had cutlery in pure gold and children were working the land to pay the country's debts.

***

Christmas has never been the same since that year. I

wish I could go back and watch my mother while eating oranges or cooking her famous sweet pies, but life goes on and we need to adapt.

These are only my memories. I haven't spoken or discussed any of it with my family before putting them into words. They might have different perspectives, maybe even contrasting memories, but I was different. I was born with a remarkable sense of awareness and discernment. I've always been a very observing human being, highly sensitive, empathetic and attentive. I don't think there are many things I forgot since I was a child in that Communism era.

Every single episode of extreme happiness or unhappiness is forever impressed in my heart and mind. I forgot stories from when I was seventeen, twenty or from last year because they didn't mean much to me. But I would never forget any childhood Christmas when my whole family, nine siblings, and my parents, gathered under the same roof and waited for Santa.

Curious is how I never ever doubted of the veridicality of Santa even though I was an extremely observant child. It is true when they say that you only see what you want to see.

***

I am alone in my rented flat, tears are flowing freely on my cheeks. I wish I could be with my parents and my family. But my siblings are living in different countries of the world, and it's not possible to meet during this time of year. We lost connection, but even so, I wouldn't want the Golden Epoch back. I want to be able to eat an orange or a piece of chocolate whenever I desire. I want to be free to travel, see the world, and get to know other cultures. I want to keep my freedom.

I could have given a party or accepted several invitations, but I do not feel like celebrating. The Communist period ended twenty-seven years ago, but I still haven't been able to step out of the curse of it. All I can think of is what door should I knock on to get an opportunity.

Maybe Santa's? People cannot understand how I can choose to spend Christmas alone. I don't know how to explain why. It's a choice as I am fighting to break the chain of countless misfortunes and discrimination. I am fighting for the right to a decent future.

They did everything in their power to make me feel like a slave again. I had no right of expressing my opinions, to use the verb *want*, to complain if something wasn't fair.

I thought I will never get out of it, but here I am today in a country that voted *Leave* (Europe), an employee of a good company who helped me grow and build some confidence and self-esteem.

I have been working for years to fix what living under a communist regime destroyed. I came a long way, but I am not where I want and deserve to be. However, I am on the right path, and I am grateful.

Merry Christmas everyone! Craciun Fericit! Buon Natale! Joyeux Noel! ¡Feliz Navidad

Cristina G.

.

Ten Years in Italy, Three Weeks a Human

Preface

This narrative is not about politics, history, or the several achievements of my small country, but about its citizens (represented by me) who are considered inferior by half of the population on this planet.

The memoir will only be of interest to the people with a human essence —people who don't consider themselves to be superior just because they were born in a developed state.

With pain in my heart, I admit that some of my friends, who are generally good beings, will not waste their time reading it because they disregard my equality to them —for the reason above. They read, however, biographies and stories about unknown individuals blessed by geography, and we talk about this all the time. I don't write for them but for those who proclaim and believe in parity of rights regardless of skin colour, nationality, heredity, or topography.

I know I shouldn't befriend individuals like that, but you cannot impose your beliefs or values on anyone. Controversy aside, some bigots are innocuous.

*

Although the following took place in Italy, I must emphasise that it could have been any other country on the globe. So, if you're Italian, please don't feel offended, I assure you that my goal isn't to denigrate your nation, but to raise awareness of unwitting prejudices that lay in many, too many of us.

I owe Italy everything I am today, and I will be forever grateful.

*

I used to think that writing from memory is an easy

task. I was very wrong.

The book was put on file in four days (from 8 am to 11 pm), time in which I relived every single memory, fear, phobia, and emotion with the same exact intensity as when it happened. The lump in my throat came back as soon as I started typing and remained with me for the entire time. Tears fled from my eyes continuously. I sweated and fought for every breath as I did for all those ten years I spent in Italy. I knew I had to write about all of them one day, but I'm glad it wasn't planned.

Names were left out to respect privacy. Besides, who would be happy to admit mistreatment, oppression, and lack of basic humanity?

The other five days were invested into correcting it, excluding the professional proofreading. After several analyses, many bits were cut to make it sound less dramatic and accusatory.

I am sorry if I hurt anyone's feelings, God is my witness that I had absolutely no intention of doing that.

*

I often talk to myself out loud or in my mind, so the single quotations mark (') are used for this dialogue.

Introduction

My name is Cristina. I came to life in the November of 1975 when my country was under a very oppressive Communist regime. My parents had other nine children before me, and a last one after me.

Born in the poorest region of Romania, Moldova, we were already considered secondary to our fellow nationals. Then again, farmers were and are the lowest class in social stratification in every country. My destiny was marked: I was to become a farmer.

For fourteen years, I lived following Communist rules, doing my duty, having no dreams... besides the one I never told anyone about. It was normality for me.

There were no documentaries or news about other nations. Our leader—Nicolae Ceausescu—was very self-centred. I was unaware of the existence of a different world besides the one I was living in. I didn't know that in other countries children had toys and played for hours every day. I couldn't even imagine that shops could be full of books, pens, chocolate, oranges, clothes, and shoes. If someone narrated stories like that, I would have laughed thinking that person had a fervid imagination.

My reality was simple and modest. The everyday life consisted of eight hours of school, six hours of working the land—or helping my mother with weaving—and feeding the animals, two hours of doing homework, one hour watching TV, eating, moving from a place to another, and six-seven hours of sleep.

When the Communist regime was defeated, and his leaders shot dead—Christmas Day 1989—I hadn't felt free because I didn't know I wasn't.

In less than fifteen hours, the country went into total chaos. The black and white TVs started to broadcast horrible footages of a war we were not prepared for. Many people lost their lives in the name of a freedom I never heard of. My brother was serving the country right in the middle of it. There were no mobiles phone back then, and we worried ourselves to death until he called a neighbour on the landline and asked to let us know he was safe. We broke down in tears, barricaded in the house and, powerless, witnessed scenes from horror movies.

The following year, I was supposed to choose and go to a high school, but there was little choice, most of them closed down after the defeat of communism. I dared to start dreaming about gaining a university degree, but it was not a farmer's destiny, so I went to a college instead.

The frontiers opened, and we were given the right to travel, but to where? No state wanted us. We were cursed by geography.

Confused for many years, I didn't know what was to be of my future, and I worried. I worried a lot. Reading, a burning desire since I discovered the letters of the alphabet, saved me from going insane. With no TV, internet, or other social activities, all my free time (mostly nights and Sundays) was invested in this passion. Devouring at least twenty books a month, by the age of twenty I had lost count of how many I actually read. However, I would never forget the first novel I read at the age of eight, *Les Miserables,* by Victor Hugo.

One day I realised that I wasn't happy with being a farmer. The hankering for knowledge, speaking another language, studying other cultures, and discovering what was beyond the communism cage, became unsustainable.

At the age of twenty-two, I decided to abandon the only reality I was familiarised with (my home, my parents, siblings, and friends) and plunge into the unknown. And I was frightened because I was a simple country girl who never saw a computer in her life.

For more than two years, I tried to get a visa to any country I could, but Italy was the only one that accepted Romanians back then. For three months I gathered various documentation. Then I went to Bucharest with a plastic bag full of papers and waited in heavy rain for more than forty hours to get inside the embassy. My application was rejected twice in a year, and I almost lost my mind because I had to start from scratch every time. The third time was the lucky one. I didn't jump in happiness, I was too fatigued, so I leant against a wall, slid down slowly, and sobbed for hours. Nobody came to ask why I was crying, everybody in there was in the same situation.

So, in August of 2000 (aged twenty-four) with a heavy heart and a small suitcase, I left my parents crying, and took my very first step into the wild world. I had no idea there was no coming back, and mostly, I wasn't prepared for what would happen after that.

Slavery at the end of 20th century

Italy was a dream and a nightmare at the same time. The Mafia was the only thing I knew about it, and I was convinced I'd end up shot or stabbed to death in the middle of a street. I took the risk anyway. If I was serious about changing my destiny, this was my only chance.

I didn't know anyone in Italy at the time. A Romanian priest helped me to find a job as a babysitter. I was to replace another Romanian who resigned from the role after a few days. When I asked her why, she said, "You'll see." I didn't know what to make of that reply, however, after a couple of hours with a deranged woman, the mother of two beautiful children, I wondered if that was what hell felt like on earth.

I am a very shy person, humble and respectful, so when that woman (blueblood descendant) cleaned the floor with my human essence, I had no power, knowledge or desire to defend myself. All I could think about was that I wished to be dead.

"Useless Romanian!" she shouted every time she saw me. "Stay out of my sight! You make me feel sick. You shouldn't have been allowed to come here."

I didn't dare to say a word, to look at her, or to even cry. I just prayed to God to take me from this world because I didn't fit into it.

One day I was writing a word on my hand because I kept forgetting in. She caught me and went ballistic. She grabbed the pen from my hand and threw it into the bin, "Illiterate creature! You didn't come here to learn, you came here to serve and follow the rules!"

I was shocked and dared to murmur, "But I need to understand what you're saying so I can follow your orders."

"Shut up! You are here because you were starving in your petty country, not to write words on your filthy hand!" she cried out loud.

My eyes blurred with tears. Luckily, my head was lowered, and she couldn't see them. I bit my lips and went to wash off the eight blue letters that got me into trouble, *straccio (cloth)*. I have never forgotten that word again.

When in bed, I couldn't sleep. The room in the basement I was given had walls covered in thick layers of green damp. It was terribly smelly. I never liked dirt. I was grateful for not being claustrophobic, but I feared I would get ill. Where could I have run from there, though?

The countess's nasty words came to mind, and I got angry. 'I was a farmer, you brute! I worked from sunrise to dawn, we had every vegetable and meat you can think of, I never starved! And I am not illiterate! Going to school is compulsory in my country! I studied from seven to fourteen and went to college for four years after that!" I shouted in my head while countless tears were finally free to fall.

Ten days later, an eternity for me, she decided to visit her family, and we were to fly from Venice to Rome. A friend of hers gave us a lift to the airport. She took one kid by the hand (the eldest, a boy) and instructed me to carry the girl and two suitcases. I had no problem with that, it was my job, but when she ordered me to walk at least one metre behind her, I felt humiliated as never before. However, thinking it was a misunderstanding, I got closer to avoid getting lost in the crowd. She stopped, pushed me hard and screamed like I was a criminal.

"Stay back, stupid Romanian! You're not on my level. Do you understand that?"

Her friend and people around looked at me with pity, but nobody said anything. I lowered my head and wondered if slavery was really abolished or it was something I only read or dreamed about.

I have never stepped into a plane before, and I used to think that I would be terrified of flying. Yet, due to my situation from which I couldn't see a breakout, I felt quite euphoric.

She had a seat in first class, of course, I didn't expect otherwise. The children stayed with me though. I took them both on my lap, looked out the window and prayed as never in my life. I begged God in my mind over and over again to make the plane crash. I prayed for me and for those two innocent children to be free of that beast.

I should have felt guilty for being so selfish, but I didn't know what else to do. I couldn't resist anymore.

As you see, there was no crash, and I survived that and infinitely more, despite my frantic prayers.

I imagined her family to be like her but they were actually nice. They invited me to sit and dine with them, but my superior (the slave owner) grabbed my hand and dragged me into the kitchen by force, locking the door twice so I couldn't get out.

The kitchen was only for cooking, there were no chairs or tables, the only space available was in front of the hobs. So, I sat on the shiny black floor, with my back against a cupboard, unable to cry. Ten days with that family, in a country famous for its food, without eating once. I just couldn't put anything into my mouth. I don't even remember drinking water. My body wasn't hungry or thirsty because my mind was petrified. Trapped… with one single possible escape, death. But I couldn't do that to my family.

When we got back, while the tyrant was resting, I went to a telephone box, and called the only Italian number I had (the priest's) and told him that I was unable to remain in the job he found me. "I prayed for the plane to crash, Father," I confessed in thousands of tears, and asked for forgiveness. He asked me not to lose hope as a friend of his would come later in the evening to pull me out of that inferno. I hadn't felt that happy in my entire life.

I went to tell her that I was resigning and ready to go back to my country. She looked at me with disgust and thought I was playing around. When she realised I was dead serious, after a second of shock, she unleashed the most brutal attack against human dignity I ever witnessed. The names she called me, the insults, humiliations, and pejoratives were unknown to me. One hour of terrifying rage in which I was a quiet listener. The avalanche of unspeakable expressions hit me with astronomical power, but I didn't blink.

While I was gathering my things, her husband knocked on my door and asked for permission to get in. I expected more abuse.

"I am mortified, Cristina," he said, "she is not feeling well. Please accept my apologies."

"Have mercy on your children," I murmured

keeping my head down. "Please take some time to observe their behaviour. The sadness in their eyes is devastating... take them away from her if you love them."

He said that her family was already taking care of the situation. I didn't know what he meant with that, and I didn't ask. I couldn't do anything for them.

When I had got there, I had had no slippers, so she had bought me a pair. I didn't put them in my suitcase because I didn't consider them mine. When I left, she threw them behind me, shouting I didn't deserve more than that.

A pair of slippers for fourteen days of hell. I didn't care about the money, I just wanted to be free.

My very first experience in Italy reminded me of *Les Miserables.* I thought it was a miracle to come out of it alive.

Deviant Love

The priest's friend and I fell in love at first sight, and that night he promised that I would never be treated that way. I believed him.

He took me to his place where he lived with his mother. A month later, the priest and the man I loved planned our wedding. I wasn't invited to the discussion. I overheard a few things I disagreed with, but I didn't intrude, just accepted my faith.

In November of 2000, still a virgin, I turned twenty-five. There was no party or cake for me. I didn't mind, 14th of November has always been just a regular day for me.

My future mother-in-law used to lock me in my bedroom every evening and took the key with her to avoid a physical union before the marriage. I wasn't bothered.

One Saturday after lunch, my husband-to-be wanted to rest and took me with him to his bedroom. The door opened suddenly, and his mother came in. I was outraged she didn't care to knock, she was horrified I was in her son's bed. The lecture she gave me was ludicrous. Her son said nothing was going on between us and demanded peace. I thought she'd have a heart attack.

A week after that, the man I loved took me on a weekend holiday in the mountains. She called twenty times in four hours, and every two hours after that. I thought it wasn't normal behaviour, but he said she loved him dearly and wasn't used having him away.

That night was my first time. I felt no pain and no pleasure either. I didn't even have a chance to think when he started to shout I wasn't as pure as I'd said. Confused and hurt I asked what was he talking about.

"You didn't bleed at all. God only knows how many men you have had inside you!"

Utterly shocked I didn't know what proof I could bring to demonstrate my innocence. Nobody in my family spoke about sex. It was a taboo subject back in my country. During the communist regime, all movies were censored, I had never seen two people kissing. And as a Catholic, I knew I had to preserve my chastity until the day my husband wanted me. I was twenty-five, but still a child, utterly ignorant in that art.

I cried for hours, and on my knees, I swore that I never, ever, had had anyone touching me before. He looked at me with profound disgust and believed nothing. We slept in separated beds that night. Upon careful reflection, I remembered reading a book about the first time—Lucrezia Borgia or something— and she bled a lot. I concluded that there must have been something wrong with my body and felt awful. I spoke to him, and with tears in my eyes, I explained my fears. I don't know if he believed me or not, but he hugged me, and we made peace. I was happy.

Two months later, while having dinner, my fiancé and his mother were having an argument about some of my fellow compatriots. It wasn't something new, quite the contrary. Not liking their allegations I ventured my opinion, 'Romanians are human too, we have the same rights as you. Why shouldn't we be allowed to buy a car if we have the money?'

Both stopped and gave me the same look and

treatment as the woman from which they saved me. "Nobody asked you anything, don't ever dare to interfere in our conversations. Just who do you think you are?" the man I was in love with asked with fury.

Despite thinking I deserved it, I went to bed crying and promising I would stay quiet from that day on.

One evening, while having a bath, I heard my future mother-in-law speaking with her son about me. The pipes from the office passed through the bathroom, and I could hear them as clearly as I was in the same room with them. The things she said nauseated me. Twenty minutes of cries and complaints about my behaviour of the day. I had no idea she hated me until that evening.

I wondered if I should say something or ignore the story. After a short debate inside my head, I chose the second variant and felt sorry for her son as I thought it must have been difficult for him to realise that his mother didn't approve of her future daughter-in-law. In a week, I heard them four times, every time I had a bath. I figured it was a regular event and avoided the bathroom after dinner again. *"What you don't know can't hurt you,"* right?

Three months later, I was in chains again. Working from sunrise to sunset, without a penny in my pocket and no right to speak, I plunged into the most profound state of misery. I knew I couldn't marry a slave owner, and serve a woman who was supposed to care for me but couldn't stand the sight of me.

On Christmas Eve, the priest came to visit and stayed for a few days. A bedroom was required, and I prepared one on the second floor. However, my future husband decided to lend his bedroom to him because was bigger and nicer. It was a beautiful gesture, a sign of high consideration and respect, and I approved of it.

That Christmas morning, I asked him which bedroom upstairs he slept in. He said, none.

"Where have you slept then? You didn't go to a hotel, did you?" I asked, surprised.

"Don't be stupid, I slept in my mother's room," he replied as it was the most natural thing in the whole world.

After a few moments of disbelief, and intense debate between my heart and brain, I asked with the calmest voice I could gather, "Are there two beds perhaps?"

"No. I always sleep with my mother when we have guests."

My face turned red from the shock, I couldn't stay silent, so I shouted with fury, "There are three bedrooms upstairs and another one on this floor, how could you choose to sleep in the same bed with your mother? My brother was five when he refused to do so. What is wrong with you people?"

"How dare you? How dare you?!" he hissed through his teeth with ire. "You're a peasant, and a guest in this country and house, you are not entitled to an opinion."

I shivered, lowered my head, and walked out of the house wandering for several hours without a destination. 'This can't be normal in any country around the globe. I am not the crazy one, they are. I can't marry a maniac and live with his crazy mother.' I thought.

One day I expressed my desire to look for a job and move away from them. He went wild, and I saw death with my own eyes, but I wasn't afraid – death was less frightening than a life with those monsters.

Eight months and I'd been a slave to the man who promised me eternal love and justice. I needed to buy some tampons, and a phone card to call home and inform everyone that the marriage was off. I went to the bank to withdraw €10. The bank account my future husband opened in my name was empty. I asked him why when he got home.

"You all come here expecting to find a panacea for all ills. Well, now you see that this is not a paradise," my ex-husband-to-be said.

"Meaning?"

"What have you done to deserve any money, except upsetting my mother in every possible way?" he replied with rage.

"I worked in the garden since I came here, helped your mother with everyday tasks. I took down walls, painted, decorated, and built a new kitchen. I organised and cleaned every inch of your three-level house that wasn't taken care of since the day you moved in, which was twenty years ago. I was your gardener, cleaning lady, builder, painter, and so much more," I replied incredulously.

He looked at me with despise, "You've done everything you wanted to do."

"I've done what was needed to be done."

"What about the bulbs, you haven't cleaned any of them!"

"What bulbs?" I asked confused.

"The light bulbs from the chandeliers."

"Is this a joke?" I shouted.

"No joke. You haven't cleaned any of the bulbs which means you only did whatever you liked to do. That's why your bank account is empty. Besides, I took you on holiday for your birthday. Have you forgotten, ungrateful woman?"

I didn't know what to say. The people were nuts.

I found a job in a restaurant where they gave me a room. He let me go saying, 'You didn't want to be a queen in this house, now you should be happy being a cleaner for all your life. People like you don't deserve more.'

I left thinking everything would be all right, forgetting I loved the brute. For eight months, I fell asleep praying for him to come after me and ask for forgiveness. And he came, but when he told me that he was thinking to take his mother to a care home, I knew I couldn't go back. The woman called and accused me of turning her son against her, she cursed and insulted me with words I knew far too well by then. I promised myself it was over and I moved on.

Sentenced to death

Two years later, I wanted to make a step towards a better profession, so I applied for a waitressing position in Cortina. I learned on the job, and because of my smile and likability, the clients loved me and looked for me. One day, a man bluntly asked why I was a waitress.

"Why not?" I replied.

"Do you know that you could be anything?" he insisted.

"Anyone could be anything," I said.

"No, not anyone, only a few. You are a rough diamond with unlimited potential. You should aim higher," he recommended.

I laughed and went back to my clients. 'I am a country girl, a farmer's daughter. I can't be anything more than a servant,' I thought in my head.

Another man told me I could live all my life doing nothing but shopping and watching movies.

"What are you talking about?" I asked confused."

'You, silly girl, utterly unaware of your tremendous sex appeal. Every man in this room has their eyes on you. Have you ever wondered why they always coming back to this place?"

"It's a restaurant, people come to eat," I replied with candour.

"They come for you," he declared.

"That can't be true, as most are married."

"So what? Fewer responsibilities for you. Rich men would buy you a house where you would wait for them and do nothing all day. They would pay for your clothes, food, holidays and so on."

I looked at him with horror. I read about stories like the one he was describing to me. "Mistress? Are you telling me that I could have a better life as a kept woman? Why would I do that when I can work and take care of myself?"

"Waitressing for twenty hours a day with €5 an hour isn't working, but slavery. You do realise that, right?"

"I used to be a farmer, this is the best job I ever had. However, I am intent on studying and building a better career," I said with hope.

"And when are you planning on doing that if you work all the time?" he asked.

"I need to send money home, I will do it as soon as I saved something for myself."

"You'll never get out of this. You're wasting your tremendous beauty and youth. Raise your head and say yes to the man over there," he said pointing to a table at the back of the restaurant.

I looked over by instinct. The man with white hair (most likely in his sixties) sat at the table alone, and was a regular client. I blushed and felt like screaming and kicking.

"I'm only twenty-seven, and I have never lived. What if I wanted to be loved?" I asked in despair.

"He could give you anything you want, he's the richest man in town."

"Can he give me a family? Can he be the one to hold me when I am scared? To help me when I need something? Can I walk with him in the streets holding hands and kissing in public? Can I present him to my family?"

"Those are the movies, girl. You live in a different

world. That's the best you can have, and trust me, it's more than most women of your country can ever dream about."

I looked at him with infinite pain. I thought he was my friend.

A week later I handed in my resignation and moved to Bologna on the pursuit of my sweetest dream, university. It was the first time I had to look for a house, and my nationality worked against me. No agency was ready to rent me a house without a job, and no private landlord I called accepted to speak with me as soon as they heard the reply to their question, "Where are you from?" I had to give up after six days of sleeping in a hostel.

I moved to Ravenna, where I was instantly hired as a waitress in a hotel where they also gave me a room to share with other girls. The owner was fascinated by my manners. He praised me in front of everyone from the start. Of course, that brought envy and hatred from all my colleagues, chefs, cooks, receptionists, waiters, waitresses; all of them despised me without giving me a chance to defend myself. I soon became a target that everyone liked to hit. They sabotaged my work, humiliated me in public, and played everyday pranks on me. I tried to discuss it with them, but they refused categorically.

"You are not better than us," they bellowed.

"I am not," I swore in tears.

"But you act like you are. The boss has eyes and ears only for you. You must have done something to have him on your side. We'll tell his wife that you are sweet on him."

I was shocked and humiliated again. That fifty-something-old man was married; his wife was always with him, and I never dared to look into his eyes. I didn't even know what he looked like. I only did my job with passion and honesty.

In less than a week, I was on to the edge of insanity. The things they'd done to me were out of this world. One day, the chef took a tray from the oven and without warning me it was hot he gave it to me. Busy with the order, I didn't notice anything. I was very thin, the iron burned my left arm to the bone, and the fingers of the right hand. I screamed in pain. Everyone was in the kitchen assisting with the planned hoax. They rolled on the floor and laughed with tears while I was in agony.

The cruelty shocked me once again. I knew I didn't belong to this world and prayed to God to take me with him. My parents, the society they lived in, the church, would have accepted a death by accident, but not a suicide. Three years of endless struggles among people who despised me only because I was born in the wrong country and zealous in my job.

I went to the boss and told him I couldn't work for him anymore. He asked me why, and I told him the truth. A phone call and in a matter of minutes later all the personnel was gathered for an urgent meeting.

"I swear to God that I'm going to fire every each of you until the last one if you don't treat Cristina with respect. She's the best employee I ever had. I could always find average workers like you, but it would take me years to find another one like her."

Astonished I looked at the man to see if he was really oblivious to the impact of that statement. The room filled with odium, I couldn't breathe. He had signed me a death sentence without realising it. I told him I couldn't stay, but he insisted and offered to transfer me to another of his hotels a few metres away. After a few minutes of intense pondering in my head, I agreed to give it a try. In the end, those people didn't know me, and I didn't know them either.

I was afraid to go into my room, and knowing that the boss was also the owner of several properties in town, I asked for an apartment for which I was ready to pay upfront. He didn't accept the money and helped me with moving right away. I left thinking I was safe.

I hadn't slept all night, and I was all shaky when I got to the new location. The treatment I received from the receptionist was the first glimpse of my new colleagues, I feared the worst. At the end of the day and several appalling pranks, I knew I was doomed. All my boss's employees knew one another for years. They were all *buddies*. I was the outsider, the enemy without intent. They were dozens against one. I stood no chance. I endured for three days when I almost threw myself off the last floor of the hotel. But I didn't want to give them satisfaction, so I resigned despite several supplications from my boss. In the end, he offered to double my salary and give me a free day a week.

"Money won't do me any good if I am dead or insane," I replied shaking like a leaf in the wind.

"But I don't want you to leave. What can I do to make you stay?" he insisted further.

"There is nothing you can do. Your employees are despicable creatures, no one can stop them. Please, don't make this harder than it is already. I am just a waitress. You'll find a substitute in no time. There is a shortage of jobs in here."

"I don't want anyone else, I want you and not only for the job. In fact, I'll let you go, but keep the flat, stay here close to me…" he begged in tears.

And there it was, the confession. The reason my co-workers detested me. They all saw something I couldn't conceive in a million years. I didn't blink, I couldn't even shout or cry, what more could I have said?

In ecstasy, my colleagues watched me walking away more dead than alive. Their faces were painted with malice and spite. I didn't want to imagine what their souls looked like. I had enough on my plate without focusing on them. 'Why is every man in this country hitting on me? Why can't I have the right to a normal relationship with any free man I chose? Can it be true that I am of inferior birth?' I refused to believe so. God created man in his own image, we were all equals.

Letizia

The stigma of being a Romanian followed me everywhere I went. There was no escape. I couldn't take my life, just move on hoping that God would have mercy on my soul one day soon. Every night I fell asleep crying, trembling, and twisting in despair. 'Please, God, make me die in my sleep. I am tired and cannot live another day in these conditions. I don't want to open my eyes again. It has never been sunny on my road. I am beginning you, my heart is sick of woe. I never liked this life anyway.'

I tried my luck in Florence where I found a couple of jobs in two very distinct restaurants and a room in a flat in front of the Duomo. My flatmates, two siblings, a girl and a boy, were having a ridiculous number of visitors, especially in the night. I thought they were very popular.

Perugia was my next location because it had an international university. A businessman (an owner of several companies) who showed me kindness years back, helped me to find a place to stay and offered me a job as secretary to the director. I refused with humbleness saying it was above my capacities. He said it wasn't, but didn't manage to convince me. I was very aware of why he'd helped me, but I ignored the fact as I couldn't find a house on my own in a city I didn't know. He was a king there, a simple phone call made it happen instantly.

I thanked him deeply, settled down in my new home, and went to the university trying to get in. I didn't have the right documentation. I gave up and followed some paid classes during the day, worked as a waitress in the evenings and weekends, and as a cleaner in the nights. I don't know if I had two hours of sleep nightly.

On New Year's Eve, when everybody was toasting and cheering, I went outside, leant against a wall, and cried my heart out. The words of that man in Cortina echoed in my head, 'You'll never get out of this.'

"Why are you weeping?" asked my boss.

"Because I have been working for three hundred and sixty-six days a year for the last five years, and lost track of time. Life is passing me by."

"Bloody Romanians. Always complaining! This is life, wake up already!" the man who paid me €4 an hour without a contract said angrily. "Go home, no?"

That animal hit on me for months without shame in front of his wife. I kept my distance and never stayed alone in the same place with him. He frightened me.

Then I thought the studies meant nothing if I couldn't get a degree. I called the businessman and asked if the job he offered me was still on the market. I had the interview the next, and a week later, I was hired part-time and kept working as a waitress on request.

In the meantime, the director of the building company I was working for, a man in his fifties (who wasn't the same businessman who hired me) was trying to get me into bed too. No surprise. I was flattered at first, and because he was nice and respectful, I tried speaking to him human to human. He always listened and agreed with my thoughts. I felt sorry for him.

Bold, short, and long-time married, of course, he

soon became obsessed with me.

His daily attentions and very personal confessions made me feel very uncomfortable and angry with him. The typical man who blames it all on his wife. So, I told him right away that I was a convinced feminist and would never partner with a man to denigrate any woman on earth. He respected me for that, at least it's what he made me believe.

I was working with him for a month when I began receiving phone calls every morning around 3. Because the number came up as private, the first time I thought that something terrible happened to my parents (my innermost fear) and almost had a heart attack. Trembling from all my muscles, I murmured "hello", but there was no one on the other end. I called home right away, nobody picked up. I couldn't go back to sleep and thought I'd die before morning, but I couldn't just ring everyone I knew in Romania at that hour. When I had managed to speak with my mother, she said that nobody called me from Romania. I calmed down and believed it was a mistake. The night after, it happened again, then again for another four nights in a row. I called my carrier and begged them to block the incoming calls from that number. It was impossible as it was a private or hidden number. The technology wasn't as advanced as it is today. I asked them for advice.

"Switch off the phone during the night," they said.

"I can't. What if something happens home and I can't be reached?" I replied in despair.

"Change the number then."

It wasn't a good idea because I never saved numbers on my phone and had no way of informing everyone about the change.

"Then you should contact a lawyer, who will communicate with the police and…"

'Contact the police? And say what? That someone plays stupid pranks on me?' It sounded ridiculous, and I dropped the case. I thought about it a lot and agreed with the first option my carrier proposed, to turn the phone off before going to bed.

I was upset and frustrated, and my boss asked me what happened. I told him a horrible creature was disturbing my sleep every night.

"Do you have any idea of who it might be?" he enquired.

"Not in the slightest," I confessed.

I don't remember what he said, I guess he sympathised with me, as usual.

The lark continued every night for at least four months. The reason I am certain of this is that sometimes I forgot to turn my mobile off, and the call was as prompt as a Swiss clock. A few times, exasperated and tired for the lack of sleep, I screamed and cursed like a pirate. The person on the other end said nothing, and just listened in silence. At some point, I thought it was an automatic prank made by a machine because I couldn't hear a human breathing. However, if it was a human, he or she must be mentally deranged. Who else would wake up in the middle of every night to call me? For what purpose?

The incident had a disproportionate impact on me because I was already suffering from stress. I didn't recover from the horrible Ravenna event. My hands were always trembling as if I was affected by Parkinson's Disease. At home, I was continuously crying. I had no TV because I couldn't afford to pay the bill, no radio or computer either. I could barely pay the rent, the bills, and the car insurance, so buying a computer was out of the question. I couldn't read as I used to. I was living an unending nightmare.

I made sure I never forgot to switch my mobile off again, so I set it to automatically turn off at 9 pm and turn back on at 6 am. That idea was a winner, and I was grateful.

One Saturday morning, around 6:05, my phone rang. The number was readable, so it wasn't the psychopath. I had no work that day and so needed to rest... I took the call, it surely was important. "Pronto?" I asked.

"Put my husband on the phone right now," ordered an angry woman voice.

"I am sorry?!" I said terribly confused.

"Don't play dumb with me!" the voice shouted. "I know he's there with you!"

I took a deep breath, everything inside me was screaming, but as calm as I could, I said, "Madam, you must have called the wrong number. There is no one here with me. I live alone."

An imperceptible pause, "I know you live alone. I took your number from my husband's phone. It's definitely the correct number."

"Who is your husband, Madam?"

Everything became clear when she said the name, my boss's name. I met her at a party a few months back. She was a beautiful woman.

"Madam, I fail to understand why you're so convinced your husband is here. He's a married man, I would never do that. I promise." Doubting of her husband, I felt sorry for her.

"Letizia," she said, "My husband hasn't slept at home once in the last four of five months. It's true that he's got a flat in the city, but I checked several times, and he wasn't there. I investigated and found out that he is obsessed with you. That's why I know for sure he's there. Now put the bastard on the phone!"

"Madam, my name isn't Letizia. You've been misinformed," I replied with hope.

"That's how he calls you. That's the name under which your number was saved on his mobile," she insisted.

I had no idea of what was going on. I was tired, angry, and offended. "Madam, I promise you on my miserable life that he is not here. He's never been inside this house. I don't fancy your husband, there has never been anything going on between him and I. If my boss is missing from home, he must be sleeping somewhere else, but I swear he is not here. Would you please clear this up with your husband, and leave me out of it? Goodbye," I said switching off the phone.

I sat on the bed and looked at the empty white wall in front of. I wanted to shout, cry, and break everything around me, but I was utterly drained of energy. I lay down on my back, staring at the ceiling for hours. I was convinced I made the last step towards insanity.

Was it my natural beauty, innocence, and humbleness that opened me every men's door, but closed all the female's ones? Or it was the sinful fame of my female compatriots the real reason behind all these infamous incidents with Italian men?

I had no concrete answer to that.

When I went to work on Monday 7:00 am, my

boss was waiting for me, smiling with all his teeth. I almost lost my temper and slapped him across his vile face. "You led your wife to believe I was having an affair with you. Why? How could you do this to her and to me?" I asked with fury. "She's the mother of your children! And I thought you cared for me as a human. What is wrong you?"

"I am sorry, Letizia…"

"Don't call me that. It's not my name!" I shouted. Luckily, we were the only people inside the small building at that hour.

"I call you Letizia because you make me happy," he replied with calmness.

"Are you mentally ill?" I shouted again. "Nothing is going on between you and me! I don't like you? Do you understand that?!"

"I understand, but I can't command my heart. You know how it is… Love…"

"What love? I am an obsession, an infatuation, not love! I thought you were an intelligent man and knew how to distinguish between these completely different feelings. How did we get here? I never encouraged you, I never even dared to raise my head and look into your eyes. You're a married man, out of the market, Goddammit! I deserve a man to love me freely, don't you think?"

"I can be that man. I told my wife everything," he said.

"What everything?! I don't want you, I don't even like you. You are my boss, a fifty-something-old married man with two children of my age. You used me to break your marriage! You're a despicable coward. I am done with being nice to you."

"Cristina," he said again. "My wife was right, I

haven't slept home any of these nights because I sat in my car in front of your house every time. What a joy seeing the light switching on in your bathroom at random hours, your beautiful silhouette walking around after a bath…"

Horrified, I looked at him to see if it was a joke. He seemed like being in a trance, or ecstasy. A mad person's look. It frightened me. Shaking from head to toe I shouted, "You're out of your mind! Stay away from me, or I'll press charges against you!"

He laughed, "Your passion is irresistible. How…"

I shivered, turned around and left his office. Mine was just the next door, but at least we were not in the same room.

Although I couldn't stand the sight of him, I kept doing my job as before. Nobody in the company was aware of our argument. His attentions and advances didn't stop, but I ignored them as well as I could.

*

Years after, when I left Italy, while telling this story to my sister-in-law, I connected the dots. The person who called me at 3 am for several months, was him, the man who said that he loved me deeply and would do anything for me. The creature who listened to my desperate stories about the maniac who disturbed me every night, and ruined the fragile layer of serenity for which I worked so hard after Ravenna. He knew how much it affected me. He was aware of my mental state, the many tears and trembling, and continued to do it anyway.

After my ex-husband-to-be, that being was the second psychopath I attracted on my path.

How could I overlook such blatant proof? Naivety. My mind wasn't able to conceive something like that. I never thought humans can be so cruel.

*** Letizia means joy, happiness, gladness.

Forever alone

I opened an account on a dating site in an extreme attempt to prove that I had someone, so he would leave me alone. My fate pushed me to meet a perfect match almost right away. And once again, it was love at first sight from both sides. Tall, smart, and kind, he was also free. Free to found a family with me. It was more than I dared to dream, and for the first time since I was in Italy, I felt happy and immensely grateful. He seemed to think the same. I moved in with him two months after our encounter, leaving the only job I loved until then, and the man who ruined it for me. My boyfriend lived almost three hundred kilometres away from Perugia; I put enough distance between my boss and us. He couldn't touch me there. I was safe.

I went to church, and on my knees, I prayed and thanked God for giving me a sign of his almighty generosity.

A couple of weeks later, in terrible pain, I went to a doctor thinking it was a sort of infection due to the lack of sexual practice. After a full medical investigation, he bluntly told me I had two diseases. "But your life isn't in danger. You will live to ninety or more," he highlighted, smiling.

"What? But I've never been ill," I asked in shock.

"Well, you are now. The internal pain is related to one disease, the external to another. Maybe they are interconnected, but these are only guesses. Nobody knows for sure."

"Have I caught these from someone?" I asked.

"No. They are not contagious. You might have been born with them."

"Genetic, you mean? My mother had eleven children, and no women in my family seemed to have any issues. It's true that sex is a taboo subject, but you can't have children if you don't have intercourse. Not in my family, at least. I never heard of in vitro fertilisation before coming to Italy."

"Then you are the first."

Everything he said was a stab in my heart.

"What can I do? There are treatments, right?"

"Not really. Both are incurable. The Pill might help a little. Painkillers will give you respite from suffering, but there are no treatments for any of your maladies. You'll have to live with them. I hope you have a very understanding husband or partner or you'd be alone for the rest of your life," was his final verdict.

'But I have had sex less than twenty times in my whole life! I've always been alone until two weeks ago,' I screamed in my head.

My body, my womanly essence, was the only thing I had. In less than five minutes I lost everything. Was it faith, God's will, or a curse? I couldn't figure it out.

I had nothing to live for. Devastated, I walked for hours in heavy rain in a city I didn't know. I paid no attention to the street signs, drivers stopped to insult me. I felt guilty for endangering their freedom and asked for forgiveness.

"Disgusting immigrant, go home already," they shouted behind me.

I ended up in front of the sea and imagined myself under the blue waves. I couldn't swim, never learned, and I was terrified of deep water.

'Do it!' my brain shouted. 'Do it, Cristina. You've lost! It's over.' But I couldn't throw myself into the cold turbid water… it's a sin. 'You're a coward and a masochist. Everything is against you. It's been this way from the start. They told you to stay in your village, work the land, feed the animals, and marry the man who proposed to you. But you refused and wanted something that isn't in your destiny. You don't live, you survive. There is no place for you anywhere. You have no home, no country, no religion, and no future… You don't deserve to be loved. You have nothing to give, not even your body. You can't bring any contribution to this world, for you can't procreate. You're of inferior birth. They are right to treat you this way. You should be ashamed for breathing someone else's oxygen!'

The man I loved called me on the mobile. I didn't know where I was. He got upset, and we fought. I cried but didn't tell him why. I blamed the city and the solitude. That night we agreed to take a break. I fell asleep on the bathroom floor, hugging the sink where I vomited until there was nothing left inside me to vomit. The next morning, I gathered my things and moved again.

The eighth time in six years. I was a dead body walking.

Exhausted, despondent, scared and alone, I settled to Conegliano, four hundred kilometres away from the man I thought was the one. I went to a doctor, showed her my diagnosis, and asked for the Pill. The Pill I have always been against for moral reasons. One hour after I took the first one, I felt sick. I thought it was to be expected. Then nausea shrouded my entire being, and I started to throw up randomly for no apparent reason. I blamed the sadness and the grief.

I looked for a job and replied to an advert in the local newspaper—a secretary position in a small private company. I was asked to go for an interview that day, immediately if possible. I lived ten minutes away, so I got dressed and got on my way. The owner, a man in his sixties, was waiting for me in crowded and smelly office. I prayed to all the gods in the universe to not make me vomit in there. He noticed my pallor. "Are you ill or pregnant?" he promptly asked.

"No," I lied.

"How long have been living in Conegliano?"

"A few days."

"Do you live with your boyfriend or husband?" he enquired.

I found the question inappropriate and said I was living with a friend.

"What do you have to offer? Tell me something that will make me hire you and not someone else," he demanded.

In that moment, I realised that was my first real interview and had no idea of what to say. I wasn't prepared for any question really and didn't know to sell myself. However, I tried with honesty, "Well, I am a fast learner."

"I don't care, what else?" he asked.

"I am devoted, hardworking, respectful…"

"You are not telling me anything that I haven't already heard from all the other applicants."

I started sweating cold. I didn't like the guy, but I did my best to find something to make him happy. "I am a reliable person, I've never missed a day of work or been late once in my life."

"Not interesting."

"No doesn't exist in my vocabulary. I don't give up easily."

"Listen, girl, what you say is useless. Everybody vaunts the same exact same lame characteristics, reliable, hardworking, loyal…"

"I agree, but how many of us are actually the way we venture?" I asked.

"I don't care!" he raised his tone.

I was tired, nauseated and upset. It was clear I was not going to convince him about my good faith, but I asked anyway, "Are you saying that you'd hire a person who misses work three times a week?"

He ignored my question. I made a last attempt, "This is my first interview. What do you want me to tell you? I am sorry I have nothing extraordinary in my repertoire. I just moved here, and I need a job. I am a great person to work with. You have my CV, call my ex-employers if you want."

He was not impressed, I walked away feeling ashamed and terribly ill. I drove for two minutes, then stopped and threw up until there was nothing left inside my stomach.

The next day, at 7 am, he called me. I was driving to go and see my sister. I didn't save his number on my mobile and didn't know with whom I was talking. Besides, I had the earphones on and didn't recognise the voice. He got upset and raised his tone. I had no doubt of his identity. "I thought about you last night, hmm…," he said.

I instantly felt sick, and I knew what was he going to say next, but I hoped he wouldn't.

"You're such a beautiful girl…"

I ended the call and blocked his number. My physical appearance opened me doors to perdition.

I applied for another job, and two weeks later, I was hired as an administrative secretary in a small employment agency. Following that, I signed up for several evening courses. In the meantime, I began the fight against my diseases despite the fact I've been told they were both incurable. I went to private clinics with expensive personnel. Four doctors in a row found nothing wrong with my body and told me upfront it was all in my mind.

"But I'm in constant pain, and intimate relationships are impossible. My skin lacerates at once, and I bleed a lot. It's unbearable, it can't be my imagination," I insisted.

"We can't help you, lady. Go back to your country if you think we are lying to you."

Five or six other medics told me exactly the same, and the conviction of being crazy had to be accepted by my mind. 'If one doctor insinuates you're crazy, he might be mistaken. If three out of are three suggest the same, you still need another opinion, but if ten of them agree on the diagnosis, you must give in. They are specialists in their field, years of studies and practice made them an authority that demands respect.'

My savings shrank considerably as every visit cost me around €100, plus the transport.

Realising that I fought a losing battle, I acknowledged my defeat and fell into a profound darkness. For months, I wandered without a purpose, walking, and working by inertia. I wrote down my feelings. Three hundred sixty-five pages filled with dejection and disturbing thoughts. When my mind refused to collaborate on writing everything I had on my soul, I took the pages printed in the library and read them carefully. So tenebrous… I was an expert in stories of all genres, but what I was reading was a pure inferno. I couldn't allow anyone to see that in me, so I burnt it down and deleted the files forever.

The nausea was my only and very loyal companion. If before I wasn't very fond of sweets, now I was utterly afraid to even look at cakes, chocolate, or ice-cream. Any odour, image of food, or just an old memory of a meal, triggered a violent state of queasiness. I soon forgot how eating without feeling sick felt like. I used to love eating, not anymore. Throwing up was a regular thing, especially in the middle of the night (while asleep) and I hated it with every fibre in my body. Pregnant women always tell disgusting stories about this, but I wasn't carrying a child. I wasn't Virgin Mary, God had no knowledge of my miserable existence.

I kept changing the pills because of these severe side effects and one day I ended up in the hospital. I didn't even remember how did I get there. The pain in my chest was unbearable, I was afraid to breathe. The purple of my lips alerted the nurses; a doctor visited me at once.

When I took my blouse off, the doctor made a step back. I looked down and said it was a rush, not contagious. "It happens when I am in tremendous distress. It will go away in a few hours."

She sighed with relief and asked me about the cicatrices on my abdomen.

"Laparoscopy," I said. I am taking the Pill in a desperate attempt to stop the disease from spreading all over my body. But I feel so sick all the time and have changed several in the last months.

"Have you started a new one recently?" she enquired.

"Last night," I replied.

"You can't take it anymore. Take a long break before trying another one. However, I strongly suggest you stop taking any, it's clear that your body doesn't like them," she decided after the investigation.

I went home and threw away several packs of pills. All of them were expensive. My family doctor thought it was safer to go with the new generations of tablets. It made sense, and I agreed, until that day when I said no more. The last one almost stopped my heart from beating. It was too risky and I decided I would go without them.

Physically and psychologically a wreck, crawling like a toddler, I couldn't remember how feeling healthy or at peace felt like. That was the bottom.

After I careful introspection, I stood up from the ground and decided to look up online to find what was wrong with me because I wasn't crazy as all of them suggested.

In a couple of days, I found several patterns to my sufferance. Many women were affected, and a doctor in Milano was known to be the absolute expert in my affliction. Eager to regain my health, I didn't care about the money and booked an appointment right away. The doctor gave me hope, and every Saturday after that, I took the 4:50 am train, had an hour of experimental treatment, and came back with the 9:35 am train. I was ready to go bankrupt and endure any painful treatment in order to call myself a woman again.

A ticket cashier once asked me, "Miss, I am

curious about your affairs in this beautiful city. I have noticed that every Saturday for the last months you take the same train to Milano and come back a few hours later. Isn't that an extremely expensive adventure?"

I looked at him surprised and said it was a business trip. Then I thought about it and realised that I didn't know anything about that city. No church, garden, or museum was familiar to me. I only knew the train station and how to get to my doctor. Nothing else. I had to focus on my treatment.

I worked alone in the office for two years in that employment agency, and I was more than happy with that. My random attacks of vomiting would have scared and disgusted anyone. No one knew about my fight. My boss, a short man in his fifties, and several of his friends hit on me incessantly.

"How come you have no children yet? The clock is ticking, tick-tack, tick-tack..." laughed one of them.

"I don't want children. Not every woman is born to be a mother," I responded with calmness.

"You're a very mysterious being," was the reply.

The allusions they made, the stories they told me, the opinion they had about the women in my country horrified me. "I went to Romania several times. I only needed a pair of tights to buy any girl I wanted regardless of age or beauty."

I felt mortified in the name of all my female nationals. No woman, in any part of the world would sell their bodies that cheap. If any of these allegations were true, it means that they lured these girls with empty promises, and after doing their dirty perversions on them gave these poor girls a pair of tights and threw them out. It's not that one can go to police and press charges when prostitution is illegal. Those men were capable of doing that and so much more. I was revolted and offended by their constant sick attentions and defamations.

One Saturday, my gynaecologist advised me to seek psychological support. "No one can make it alone," he said.

His kindness moved me. He was the first Italian to treat me as a human being. Since I was a child, I thought psychiatrists, psychologists, hypnotherapists were a bunch of thieves and deceitful creatures. Despite the scepticism and aversion towards that specialisation, I listened.

There was a private practice five minutes away from my office, I called and booked five sessions. When I got in and looked throughout the bookshelves, I realised I had read them all. I told her that right away.

"Then you know everything I know."

I started with the left foot, we didn't connect.

"I hadn't realised you are not Italian when we spoke on the phone," she said.

"I have lived in Italy forever... it seems to me," I replied with melancholy. "I speak better Italian than Romanian. I love your language."

She didn't look impressed. However, I told her about my dream, "I came here to fight against my destiny. I think I have the right to want more from life. I can do better than this. I had no opportunity in my country. No hope."

One day I met her in front of my office. The street was deserted, so I said, "Good afternoon." She pretended not to see me. I was baffled. When I questioned why did she ignore me, her reply was simple, "You are just a patient."

On the sixth appointment, I was crying because of my boss's advances. As usual, she listened without intervening once. I asked for advice.

"Changing career?! Looking for a waitressing position? There are loads of restaurants that need personnel," she said.

"I have invested a lot in my studies, I would like to find a job in which I could use my skills."

"You won't find any. Aren't you aware of the reality around you? Companies are closing down every day. Many Italians are without work. You should look for a position that is on your level. Like a carer or babysitter."

I felt like screaming and kicking. Instead, I bowed my head thinking I was right not to trust her. When the session was over, I told her I wasn't going to come again. She didn't blink.

"What about going home and helping your parents with the land?" she insisted after I paid.

I ignored the slap in my face and promised I would never, ever spent another penny on psychological support. That woman should have never been allowed to practice.

One day, I discovered by chance that my boss has never paid the required taxes for the employees, myself included. Two years of pension contributions lost like I had worked without a contract for all that time. I handed my resignation in right away, and the insults were quick to arrive. I felt nothing, my skin was thick enough to take them.

My gynaecologist sold me a very expensive device and told me that I was in a place where I could continue the treatment at home. I felt profoundly grateful and optimistic.

A broken thumb, a shattered mind

I moved three times after that, the last one to a small village. I needed peace and quiet, and for the first time since I was in Italy, I thought that it would be better to give up to the foolish dream of changing a destiny that was already written and signed. As my mother use to say, "Whatever happens at all happens as it should." But I couldn't give up. My parents wanted me home, of course. However, there was nothing for me to do in Romania, except for the land.

It took me a long time to find a house, as soon as I confessed I was Romanian, landlords usually washed the floor with my dignity or simply closed the call. In three months, I lost a considerable amount of money on rentals that didn't suit me until I found the right one. The landlord told me upfront that he despised my compatriots—all immigrants really without distinction— but he was a business person. I had nothing against that and settled down.

Later, it came up that my landlord had lived in France for four decades and came back to Italy the year before at his wife insistences. It was a paradox the way he felt about the ones like him.

The house was huge but lacked central heating, and the windows were all faulty. The wind was howling everywhere. I tried to tell my landlord that it was a big problem, he said he didn't care. I spoke with a friend about it, he offered to help me for free. Half of the day we worked and insulated the eight huge windows as best we could.

"I won't pay for anything you do in the house. But

you'll pay highly if you break a single bulb," the landlord shouted when he came to inspect the house due to the movement he noticed inside.

I didn't reply, I knew that already.

Three plastic bottles filled with hot water became my nightly companions.

One evening, I couldn't breathe. A pain in the right side of my upper body made me think the worst. I drove to the hospital and waited patiently in line. Another pain in my lower abdomen added to the first one. I thought it was the end, but I was upset. 'Why do I have to suffer this much on my last day on earth? One day you refused to give me, God, a single peaceful day. Even you treat me as an inferior birth.'

Tears of frustration rolled down my face. When a woman doctor called my name, I almost couldn't stand up and walk. I bit my lip and gave myself a kick.

In her room, without even looking at me, she ordered me to take off my clothes and explain the symptoms.

I did my best to be clear, but my voice trembled and the tears refused to stop falling.

"You useless immigrants, coming to the hospital for every headache to spend our money," she hissed through her teeth while pressing with force on my abdomen.

I screamed in pain. The look she gave me froze the blood in my veins. I was convinced she'll kill me with the stethoscope.

"Get up and go pay the ticket. Tell me your name and date of birth," she shouted.

"Cristina G., 14 November 1975," I murmured more dead than alive.

"Hmm. Today is your birthday. Instead of

celebrating you came here wasting my time."

In a trance, I took the piece of paper she handed me with wrath, walked out the room and leant against a wall not knowing what had happened and where to go. I was all shaky and felt like fainting. Thousands of tears continued to roll from my eyes. 'My birthday,' I murmured. 'Today is my birthday.'

A middle-aged nurse came to ask me if I was okay. I was afraid to speak, I was afraid to even breathe. "I... I ne..need to pay for..for the visit, but... I do...do..don't know wh...wh...ere to go," I startled.

"Come with me, I'll show you," she said with kindness. Sustaining my weight, she took the paper from my hand. "It's your birthday today," she said with a smile. "Listen, you don't have to pay right now. You can go home and wait for the bill to get there, okay?"

I nodded "Yes," and murmured "Thank you," and walked outside the building swaying dangerously on my feet. I sat in my car and cried until the tears dried out. Then I switched on the engine and made a solemn promise to never walk into a hospital again unless I was dead.

At home, I took a small piece of paper and wrote down in four different languages these words, "If you read this because you found me unconscious, I beg you, don't call for help. Let me die in peace. God bless."

Ten years after, I can sincerely tell you that I kept my promise and still carry a request of that sort in my wallet.

I stayed in bed twisting in agony for two days, then the pain disappeared. My savings were long gone, my brother helped me every month, but I couldn't continue that way. I needed to look for a full-time job.

The next day I was hired in a wood factory, and another chapter of dreadful treatment began. If before my bosses weren't despicable to me until I refused their advances, in here, my team leader took up on me at first sight.

Every time he passed me by, my name was shouted with rage. I was outraged and couldn't find any plausible explanation to that extreme behaviour.

At first, I thought it was my imagination. I blamed it all on my past experiences. I tried to convince myself that he wasn't mean to me, he was just a violent tyrant with everyone. However, my co-workers confessed that although he was indeed a bully and many women pressed charges against him, he has never treated anyone so appallingly for fifty days in a row.

I wondered why was he still allowed to work among people? Why wasn't he in prison if so many people pressed charges? The answer was self-explanatory, his victims were all immigrants, and the owner of the company was his brother.

One day, unhappy with my productivity, he grabbed my right hand, squeezed it hard and pressed on the piece of wood I was scraping on, to guide my movements. My fingers were already in a lot of sufferance for that wasn't a regular factory. Pure and plain exploitation of man by man. The pain was unbearable, and I fought to be left alone. My thumb turned purple, and blood came out of it in waves. In agony, I looked at him to see why. His mischievous smile froze the blood in my veins again. Evil. I was convinced that if he had a gun, would have killed everyone in sight. Including his brother. I thanked God it wasn't America.

I kept on working despite the excruciating pain in my thumb. At home, I put it on ice to have some respite. When the swelling went down, I could see the nail broken at its root, under the skin. Or was it the bone? I wasn't sure. Something was fractured under my skin. That beast crushed my thumb. A form of torture used on terrorists.

I had a fever for many hours after I took a couple of painkillers, and trembled uncontrollably despite the three plastic bottles filled with hot water in my bed. I don't think it was because of the physical pain, but of the moral one. I was afraid to go back to work, to see that devil again. No one could work with a broken thumb when that was the most important part of the body to do the job.

After hours of anguish, I realised with horror that the fault must be mine. I was emanating signals to demented creatures everywhere I went. I heard of hapless humans like me. I thought there was something written in invisible ink on my forehead, that only utterly sick individuals could read, "Here is your victim."

I didn't know what to do. 'Should I go the labour union? Do we even have one? Immigrants, I mean. Maybe to the police, to a priest, or just cut my veins and end this misery?'

I vomited a few times and fell into a restless sleep.

The next day I went to work although my entire being screamed in terror. I hid my struggles under a mask pretending all was well, but I was on the edge of insanity. My thumb was broken, and my mind was shattered in billions of tiny pieces. I wasn't sure I would ever be able to put them back to make a whole. I needed the money to pay the rent, the mortgage on my car, and send some home, I was not going to lose it. I didn't have that right. I was of inferior birth, that was my destiny.

Besides my job in the factory, every weekend, and random evening or celebrations, I worked as a waitress to get back on track. But my hands were trembling so hard that I couldn't carry a cup of cappuccino without spilling half of it. The sound made by the cup hitting against the saucer attracted attention to me all the time. I had to concentrate on my hands and prayed God to make it stop as it was very embarrassing. My face was constantly red, and I was afraid to speak to anyone as I also began to startle.

I was terrified to go to sleep because I didn't want to wake up and go to work and meet that beast.

For seven months, I quivered and cried in terror and despair every single night until one morning when I couldn't take it anymore.

At 6:57 am, before the start of my working day, that demon shouted at me without reason, as always. I waited until the HR staff arrived and handed in my resignation letter which I carried around for all that time.

"But why, Cristina? You just signed another six-month contract," the head of HR asked.

I told her everything. She turned red, pressed a button, and asked my team leader to present himself in her office right away. I wasn't prepared for that.

He came smiling and joking. She ordered silence and exposed the problem.

He laughed and said I was exaggerating, he wasn't treating me worse than others.

"Worse than who?!" the head of HR asked. "You mean that other employees are in this situation? Is this the reason so many people don't last more than a week in here?"

I didn't know the woman, but those questions made it clear she was oblivious of his behaviour, or maybe she was a fairly new acquisition of the company.

"She's got two jobs," my team leader said suddenly.

The woman looked at him in disbelief, my shock was even greater.

"What has that got to do with anything?" she shouted.

"You know, she works all weekends and many evenings during the week," he insisted.

"Are you insinuating that Cristina is not doing her job properly? The only person in this company who's got a diploma in woodworking?! Then how come it has come to my ears that the other team leaders have been fighting over her since the day she started working in here? Only last week I got two requests of moving her. And the week before, and the other one again. Everybody wants her on their team, but you opposed with vehemence to her transfer! I thought it was because you considered her an irreplaceable asset to your team. But now I understand the reason behind it!" The woman was furious. "You're making this company losing excellent employees and loads of money. You're a plague, and I will do everything in my power to remove you from your duties as soon as possible," she promised.

The evil man lost his wicked smile. My heart was about to come out of my chest, I could barely breathe. That confrontation opened my eyes. The woman ordered the monster to leave her office and asked me to reconsider.

"As long as he is still allowed to lead people, I can't and won't do that," I said convinced.

"What about working in a different team?"

"I would still meet him and hear his voice yelling at people for no reason."

"It's difficult to find a job nowadays," she insisted.

"It's been like this for years and managed to survive. I will be fine."

"I know you will," she said in the end. "Cristina, I am truly sorry that you're leaving. Please remember that if you ever wanted to come back, there is always going to be a place for you here."

I thought she would apologise for his behaviour, but she didn't. I wasn't disappointed.

My contract stated that I had to give two weeks' notice before leaving, which meant I had to see that monster for another ten days. I was convinced he will kill me in that time. 'If only he has a gun and make it quick,' I thought in despair.

The day went on without further abuse from the evil. I went home trembling like a leaf and slept nothing that night like many others before. I so wished not to go back the next day, but I had to. Ironically, he was nowhere to be seen, the assistant team leader took his place; I was in heaven. A week passed without the sight of the demon. Rumours were going around, it appeared that what he's done to me was the last straw that broke the camel's back. I was happy for all the employees. That thug should have been put in a straightjacket and locked up for eternity.

In the meanwhile, all the other team leaders and the director of the factory came to talk to me about my resignation. "Reconsider, Cristina. Italy is not going well, it's difficult to find a job," they all advised me.

"Was the beast fired?" I asked.

"No. He can't be fired, he's the brother of the owner. He's been sent home for a while. However, he's already been transferred to a different department. You will not take orders from him again," the director assured me.

"I don't mind taking orders from anyone, and you know it well. The chance he'll come back is always present, right? When the new boss is on holiday, ill, or can't come into work. Besides, I might have to work directly with him when these two departments share the same project," I said.

"You're probably right, but we'll protect you," he insisted.

"And how are you planning on doing that? Hiring a bodyguard? You know you can't guarantee my safety," I said with sorrow. "My decision is taken, and only God knows it wasn't an easy one, I am tired of changing jobs, but there is no other way for me."

I left despite the tangible worry that I wasn't going to find anything full-time and with a contract. But regaining my health was more important than money. I was prepared to sleep under a bridge or throw myself into the sea. I reached the ultimate level of degradation, both physically, psychologically, and spiritually. If before I used to criticise and deny that phobias were real maladies, I realised that I developed quite a few and they were incredibly invalidating. I fell into a profound state of desperation. I accepted the fact that I didn't deserve to have a relationship or to be loved. I was fine with the shopping phobia (Officinaphobia) because I had no money anyway. The problem was that I couldn't even pass in front of a shop. It made me feel physically sick, and I couldn't breathe. I was also fine with Doctorphobia, the fear of needles and injections (Trypanophobia), the fear of hospitals (Nosocomephobia) because I interrupted all contacts with the medical world. But the fear of going to work (Ergophobia) was utterly killing me. On top of that, I was terrified of people (Anthrophobia) therefore, I couldn't even get out of the house without sweating, trembling, and vomiting.

All these irrational fears made me feel guilty, ashamed, dirty, crazy, and unworthy of any act of kindness from anyone. I was a human relic, but I went to look for a job anyway. I couldn't afford to stay in bed and stare at the ceiling. Beings like me don't have the right to grieve.

I found a day job in a factory and kept working as a waitress on request. Every second of my life was a battle. I fought to get up, walk outside the house, drive, speak with people, go to bed, eat. Nobody knew what I was going through as my face always smiled and looked down. I was exhausted in every imaginable and unimaginable way. Every step I took was by inertia. So were the breaths.

The day my phone rang with the request of waitressing for the whole winter holidays, something broke inside me irredeemably. I started crying and trembling even harder than before. I didn't know it was possible. A lump in my throat, I couldn't breathe.

My heart was about to explode. The cruel reality hit me with astronomical power.

I was thirty-two, with absolutely nothing in my hands, and even less at the horizon. I had two or three jobs and worked for eight years, sometimes for twenty-two hours a day without a single holiday. I had no slice of social life, no fun, no TV license, no laptop, not even a damn camera. 'The fight against my destiny has come to an end,' I murmured. 'I can't win versus the universe, God, or other powers I don't know about. I was born a farmer, and I will die a farmer.'

I took the car, drove for hours without a destination until I found an empty spot above a hill. I stopped and prepared to jump into the chasm. But I hesitated and fumbled… again.

I was afraid I wouldn't die, but break my neck, or spine and become disabled for the rest of miserable existence. 'Coward!' I shouted in my head. 'Good-for-nothing you are.'

I fell to my knees and screamed until I lost my voice. Then I cried, and cried, and cried… It was deep night when I got back.

If you'd ask where was that place and how did I get home, I wouldn't know what to tell you. I was utterly oblivious to the surroundings. I still see the scenery in front of my eyes from when I was about to jump, but that's all I can remember from that journey into the depths of insanity.

After the discovery of my maladies and my desperate attempt to fix the unfixable, I avoided any intimate relationship with any men. I went on a few dates, but they didn't work out. My gynaecologist recommended me to try and find a suitable partner to test the efficacity of the treatment. He assured me that the skin of my intimate parts regenerated and seemed to have regained the normal elasticity, but I was too scared. I used to shiver only at the idea…

Besides, I am not the type to have sex just for the sake of it. Feelings were and are an absolute must for me. However, I would have never known the treatment worked if I didn't try. So, I had to impose on myself to open my heart after four years of seclusion. The worst part was that I never went anywhere besides work.

So, in my last waitressing period in the mountains (Dolomites – Cortina) I met many famous and influential people and a ski instructor. I don't know, but usually, when women think of a man who teaches skiing, they imagine a tall, tanned, sporty, and very handsome creature—maybe not very smart though—no one is perfect.

Well, this ski instructor was everything *but* the above. However, because he was my age and with no string attached, I fell for him. My self-esteem was zero, I was the easiest prey.

His behaviour was deplorable from the start. I tried to speak to him from human to human, and he laughed in my face. But he complimented my intelligence, beauty, and cooking skills. I grabbed onto those first recognitions of my worth like a baby to his mother's breast.

One day he proposed I get into business with him. I sat down and listened.

"Let's open a holiday farm. I bring in clients and entertain them; you cook, take care of the house, feed the animals, and work the land. Your recipes and simplicity will enchant everyone," he explained with excitement.

Thinking it was a joke, I laughed my socks off. He got so offended. I apologised and made him aware of the flaws of his plan. "Would I have someone to help with all these activities?" I asked.

"We wouldn't earn anything if we had to pay someone," he replied.

"You do realise that I have two hands and the day has twenty-four hours for me too, right?"

"I observed you in action several times. You can cook a very rich dinner for seven people in twenty minutes or less. You are very organised and practical. In two years, our farm would find its way to success."

I said I wasn't up for it and went to bed crying. There was no point insisting that I was tired of working to make other people dreams possible to the detriment of mine. He was very disappointed.

This guy wasn't disrespectful to me because I was Romanian, but because I was a woman. Someone taught him that women were born to serve the man without discussion. I was not going to fall into that game, I was doing everything in my power to get out of it.

The fights between us were shameful. I tried to speak to him, he didn't want to listen. I shouted, he turned around and left. I sent him texts, he never replied. There was no shred of dialogue. Things had to be done the way he wanted, or not at all. My freedom was in front of the hob when I was with him. He never interfered with my cooking, and I was grateful for that.

As I mentioned, he was not a very good-looking man, quite the contrary. The way he dressed made you think he had something missing inside his head, the brain. He could not coordinate his outfit. We were antipodal in every single way. Despite my internal turmoil, my external appearance was neat and elegant. I was easy on the eye.

One day, we went for a day trip in Austria and sat for a cappuccino outside a bar. We haven't seen each other in a very long time, and I was telling him how much I missed him. Just in the middle of this romantic conversation, the man who admitted that I was the love of his life, makes a trivial remark on a woman with a very short skirt.

I looked at him in disbelief and asked him how he could be such a jerk.

"What? All men dribble over short skirts and tight outfits. It's instinctive. I am not going to be a hypocrite and hide it. I am an honest man, baby."

I got up and left. The problem was that my bag was in his car. After wandering around for fifteen minutes to calm my heartbeats, I had to go and search for his vehicle.

When I got there, the lecture he gave me made me throw up. I couldn't believe that a human can be such an animal. I did my best to explain to him that it wasn't honesty, but lack of respect. "Women are not as stupid as you think. We know you look at any female who's got something to show, but we ignore your animal instincts so we could live in peace. What you've done is simply unacceptable." His perspective was different, of course, so he decided I was a snob and very demanding.

I told him that I hated the fact that I was so much into him despite the shortage of positive attributes in his character and personality. But he already knew what I thought, I never made a secret of any of that.

From this last love story, I (thought) learned one crucial thing, '*It's better to be alone than in bad company.*' — George Washington.

*

The expiry of the residence permit gave me loads of issues. The bureaucracy was very demanding. The risk to be sent home for a reason or another was always behind the corner. For months, I had to control the extreme levels of stress. To avoid missing a day of work, I lost many nights in front of these special police departments (quaestorships). Armed with patience and high thresholds of tolerance, many times I waited outside praying to God to make the process go smoothly. Everybody was abused in one way or another. The people working in there made use of a very aggressive tone, their manner of asking questions sounded like accusations. But you had to keep your head down and reply with humility.

Unfortunately, I must admit that in my country happens exactly the same. People in charge with anything treat the ones in need with disregard and antipathy.

Once, after seven hours of waiting outside in the cold, I started vomiting and crying from frustration and tiredness.

Someone, probably a bodyguard or doorman, came to ask why such extreme behaviour. I said that I was tired of being treated like a criminal all the time.

"What did you expect? Italians to kneel in front of you and praise your presence in the country? Who do you think you are?"

"No, I expected their treatment to be directly

proportional to *my* actions. I work, pay taxes, follow the rules. I represent one honest person, not a bunch of misfits. I would like good people to be distinguished from bad people. I don't think it's too much to ask. Respect is a right that everyone should have until they do something to lose it. I have never broken the law, and I am a hardworking person."

*

This is not everything I went through while living in Italy. Most of my medical history was left out on purpose. Way too painful. When I made a tally of the money I invested on my health, the final amount (including the transport, and the days I couldn't go to work due to a couple of surgeries) was around €25,000. What I saved in six years (having more than one job and no holiday) I spent in less than two. Of course, to this I added the help from my brother and the income earned in the last years I worked in Italy (10 years in total). However, I cannot prove this ludicrous sum because more than 90% of the private visits were not billed.

Everything happens for a reason

It was time to go back home. I left Romania because there was nothing for me in there; eight years later, I was feeling the same about Italy. However, because of some unexpected issues, I was forced to remain in the country, where I lost my all my hopes, health, and virginity for two more years. Parts of me screamed and insisted on throwing myself in the abyss of the Adriatic Sea to avoid being ridiculed in my country, 'You are too old to be single. Everybody will point their fingers at you. The gossip will destroy you and your parents.'

Deciding between suicide or mockery wasn't easy, as I was a coward, but in June of 2010, defeated in everything, without a shred of dignity left intact inside me, I went home.

My family expected me to build an enormous house, as most of my compatriots who had left their country for a better and decent future had. Neighbours, old friends, and random people I had never met or known came to borrow money from me for many months. Every bachelor or divorced man in close and not-so-close proximity began courting me.

I, utterly broke and broken, smiled and pled to be left alone with my thoughts.

Accepting defeat is never easy, but being forced to admitting crash by geography and destiny, can't be expressed in the words we humans have already invented.

I wished I could tell someone what has happened. Why I was still single at thirty-four, and why I came back without a penny in my pockets. But who would have believed me? I tried a few times, they laughed in my face. I groped in the dark, breathed and walked by inertia in absolute solitude for several months, but I knew I had to rise one day.

I started working with my mind (or against it) to reach a level of serenity that allowed me to keep breathing. I thrived to build thin layers of self-esteem, confidence, and dignity that were so easily destroyed by beings without humanity.

Despite my fear of people, I forced myself to walk in the park of my city every time I was home. I also forced my eyes to see and enjoy the green, the flowers, and the trees.

I helped my parents with the land and learned to survive with €15 a month (except the bills).

You might think that isn't a big deal, that anyone can do that in a country like Romania. Well, you have to think twice as the prices in my country are almost the same as in Italy or England (sometimes even higher). However, I didn't have a rent to pay, no TV license, or other non-vital things. The only money I spent were on the internet connection, and the bus tickets when I went to visit my parents (every week for three or four days).

The internet connection was the most important thing for me as I needed to research and learn how to regain my dignity. And at the insistence of my brother, I started blogging to keep my mind busy. But this is another story.

*

Seven years after I left Italy, I look back and know that everything happens for a reason. Please make a note of the fact that I would *never, ever,* affirm that all

Italians are like the ones I met. That will mean going against everything I stand up for: discrimination, injustice, narrow-mindedness, arrogance. In fact, some of the creatures with a say in this inferno (mostly co-workers) had different nationalities, Romanian was one of them.

I have very good friends in Italy, with whom I kept in contact to the day. One is due to visit me soon, and I am over the moon.

Two people (with important functions) treated me as a human in all those years, the Milano gynaecologist (internationally renowned) and a hotel director from Asiago.

The hotel in Asiago (a small town in the Alps) where I waited tables for three weeks, was the only workplace where my colleagues and superiors were almost all humans. The only place where I was treated and paid appropriately.

My love for one of the most beautiful countries in the whole world has been severely damaged because of my experiences with the many people I encountered on my path.

I came to terms with the abuse received from creatures such as my wood factory team-leader who was illiterate, and most likely, psychopathic. But the psychologist, several doctors, a couple of directors, and some businessmen, were highly educated individuals, how should I explain their behaviour towards me?

*

Would you like to know why have I had two or three jobs, or have you already decided that I was a greedy Romanian (like all the others you know)?

No, I am not a workaholic, although I have

worked almost without a break since I can remember.

If I told you that I would have very much enjoyed lying in bed and reading every book ever written, would you believe me?

What would you do if you didn't have to go to work?

The reason I had more than one job at a time was from the desire to build a future for me and a decent house for my parents. A house with running water and an inside bathroom with a shower.

To the day, my parents still use a toilet that is ten metres away from the house. And winters are harsh in Romania. The temperatures often go below 20 or even 30 °C.

They don't have a shower every day, they wash their hair and have baths in plastic bowls.

Sacrificing for people we love is what makes us human.

*

At the end of this painful memoir, and because I decided to forget and forgive, when I say Italy, my thoughts go to Asiago.

When I speak about Italian people, I think of my gynaecologist, a few friends, and a bunch of people from the Asiago hotel.

God bless all these people, especially the Asiago ones, who in three weeks charged my batteries with their kindness, so I could wipe off the first five years of mistreatment and last for another five years in hell.

When people hear me saying that I lived in Italy, they envy me. I would feel the same if I had a different story. Italy is a dream for many people. As it was for me too.

I love art, and I'm very fond of opera (classical

music) and paintings (Renaissance, Impressionism periods). A grand part of the world's art is in Italy, but I have seen just tiny bits of it in my short breaks of serenity. I lived in Florence but didn't manage to visit *Gli Uffizi…* I have no recollection of Milan, Bologna, Rome and so on. The dark inside my soul covered my sight.

Out of this mishap, I have two things to be tremendously grateful for, the language and Prosecco. *God save the Prosecco!*

Would I do it again?

Absolutely! If I had remained in Romania, I would most likely be married and tied up to my fate. Despite all physical, psychological, and moral abuse, my present situation is only possible due to my permanence in Italy. My frequency has changed significantly since then.

It goes without saying that I would have preferred to be spared at least half of the above, but I survived, and now I have great tales to tell the world. Others are not so lucky.

This is my true story and regardless of all the precautions I've taken, I am getting ready for the negative feedback that it will receive. Being a blogger for six years taught me something, *'Despite all your efforts of being grammatically and politically correct, some readers will hate everything you say. = You cannot please everyone.'*

However, one can never be adequately prepared for gratuitous abuse.

Every tree has dry twigs

I would very much like to establish that Romanian is not synonym with humans of inferior birth. And it's not synonym with stupid, thief, or lawbreaker either.

My country has natives like the ones I mentioned, of course, but which nation could affirm that its population is free of crooks, prostitutes, thieves, and illiterates?

If one Italian is a mafia member, does it mean that all Italians are mobsters?

If one British is alcoholic, does it mean that all British have a problem with alcohol?

If one American is called Trump, does that mean that all Americans are Trumps?

If some dishonest Romanians live on the benefits of any foreign country, why should I be the one to pay for that?

Every tree has dry twigs. And you, intelligent person, know that very well. One cannot be held responsible for others' crimes. Don't punish an entire nation for the delinquencies of a few.

How would you feel being accused of dishonesty when all your life you strove to be correct with everything and everyone?

Nobody asked my fellow compatriots or me if we wanted to be born in Romania, a country in the Eastern Europe.

The fact you were born in the UK, USA, Italia, Canada and so on, doesn't give you the right to consider yourself superior to my nationals and me, it only means you were luckier.

I don't know who decided and where, but until we get a straight answer, I affirm with pride that I am just as human as you are.

Every person born on this planet, regardless of the geography, is human.

There are no superior or inferior births. God made us all in his own image. And when I say God, I mean the Universe, or whoever or whatever created us.

I don't need to urge you to discover how America became what is today? Do a simple research on the internet. What does it say about the inhabitants of those lands? Where are they now?

What about Canada, France, Russia, Germany, etc. etc.?

What do you know about Romania? Dracula? Transylvania?

Honestly?! It's better than nothing. I don't really expect anyone to have any knowledge of my small country. Why would you? History is not compulsory. I don't know much about yours either as I loved literature more than history.

However, I would like to tell you that Romanians have always lived on the land that belonged to them since God knows when.

We never aimed or attempted to occupy other nations (despite the Hungarians' allegations), but we've often been attacked and enslaved.

Our anthem explains the history of my country in depths. Fight, Freedom, and Worth are the main messages in it.

Romanians speak a Romance language, and we are proud of our Latin origins.

I won't make a list of names of illustrious Romanians who made an enormous contribution to the progress of the humankind because this is not that type of book, this is my life.

A life of a person born on Earth. Just like you.

Great Expectations

I live in England now (May 2017).

When I moved here in June of 2014 helped by a British friend (woman), I was still in recovery from the Italian's story. My friend gave me shelter, fed me chocolate, and took me to visit the amazing places around Exeter. I have never seen so much green in my entire life and fell utterly in love.

When people speak about the UK, they say rain—wet. When I talk about the UK, I say rain is green—a synonym of life. And I also say that if you do your job, follow the rules, and mind your own business, you can earn an honest living in peace. Here you can see women building houses, driving trucks, and cutting wood with the ease of a man.

People smile and compliment your achievements. Men date foreign women regularly and treat them with equity. Nobody expects you to be a slave.

I can never thank my friend enough for her infinite kindness. How can I ever repay her for the new chance to continue the fight against my destiny? The possibility to pursue my dream of a decent life? My heart is filled with gratitude and appreciation.

When the Brexit Referendum had the notorious outcome, my shock was planetary. Nobody treated me with disrespect here, and without a TV, radio, or discussions on this theme, I didn't expect this in a million year.

That fatidical day I woke up at 4 am and got ready for studying English. I switched on the laptop and Google prompted me to check the results. 'I already know the results,' I thought. 'People can't…' *What?!!* I felt like I had been struck by lightning out of the blue.

In nanoseconds, I saw history repeating itself and fell terribly ill. But I imposed myself not to take it personally. 'It's not my country, I can only be a spectator and respect their decisions.'

I work and pay taxes in here, but I am afraid and worried for my future as I have finally managed to start pursuing my childhood dream. After all the battles I had to fight against my will for so many years, I am too fatigued. I still have wounds that need to be cauterised. I still tremble and cohabit with irrational fears.

I am due to start gathering the documentation to prove I deserve to stay in here. I understand it's the law, and I am going to be cool about it. The bureaucracy was scandalous in Italy… So many days, weeks spent in queues from 1 am… I hope it won't be the same in here.

I can't ask for the British citizenship as I don't have the required years of residence. But do I want to have a British passport?

Brexit went through because most people voted against immigrants. Should I impose my presence in a country who wanted me out?

Do I feel guilty for living here?

In Italy, Romanians were hated because they were accused of stealing the Italians' jobs. However, the country lacked carers, builders, and farmers. These jobs are the hardest, and Romanians were happy to earn an honest living.

Why were we accused of stealing these jobs that no Italian wanted, I don't really know. I guess people always need to blame somebody for things they can't or don't want to figure out.

You ask any Italian if she/he's okay with living for twenty-four hours a day with an old person affected by Alzheimer's. If he's okay with having no free days, often with no contract, no daily showers, no heat in the room, little food, a miserable pay, and an outrageous treatment.

I will wait here until you get a "Yes." But I won't live forever.

Last year I discovered that Romanian hospitals are packed with women (and men) who worked in these conditions (or even worse) for many years. Some of them are my sisters.

I believe that I have all the rights to be here. I am not doing the job of an English. Unless this British speaks both Italian and Romanian and would like to do my job.

If so, please do get in touch, I will gladly step back and hand you my headphones… if my company agrees to it, of course.

*

Great Britain doesn't owe me anything. No one owes me anything. But forgive me if I cry for a chance to pursue my dream. I don't care from where it might come. I am ready to move anywhere to be able to make a living from writing. I will learn a new language, discover a new culture, and make new friends. Because I only live when I write.

I am forty-one-years-old and have nothing but this dream. I have been walking on this path since I learned to read. Despite the lack of a PhD, the curse of the geography, and the countless humiliations, I dare to say that being a writer is my destiny.

I don't ask for charity, I ask for fairness.

'What doesn't kill you makes you stronger.' is a statement I disagree with. Everything negative that happens in your life erodes your serenity and pushes you into an abyss of excruciating pain.

Everyone has two choices in this life, to give up or keep on going. But often, keep on going is too difficult when good avoids you, and many lose their minds.

When everything and everyone is against you, isn't death the only and right choice?

God Save the Queen and the English breakfast!

The funny bits–Cortina

I worked twice in Cortina. My seasonal waitressing career started and finished there. From the first experience, there isn't much positivity to write about. I met quite a few celebrities, but that never had any importance to me. VIPs are people just like us, just extremely rich and famous, of course. Some were quite rude and arrogant, not all though. It would be unfair to generalise.

In 2007, my last seasonal experience, I worked for a very posh restaurant that was, somehow, in the Michelin Guide. The only restaurant from that area to have that privilege.

I know you're curious, but I'm sorry I can't reveal the name. Contrary to Asiago's hotel, I *don't want* to make them free publicity as they have absolutely no merit in front of my eyes. If you ask me if I thought it deserved the notoriety and the stars, I would say *absolutely not!* But that is only because of the owners— my employers—who exploited and humiliated me behind my back every day. Never in my face though. Anyway, there is a funny story I'd like to write about.

The reason I was hired was that I spoke English (sort of). The guests were 80% foreign people. Russians mostly, but also Arabians, and extremely important political figures from around the world. I served quite a few heads of states and numerous huge celebrities. I am not sure it's something to be proud of. In fact, I am not. I mentioned that just to highlight how big was that place. Not big in size, but in reputation. The heads of states were very polite, their staff not that much. Despite that, we had some guests with a modest income. They spent maybe a week salary for a lunch, but I guess they thought it was worth it.

Russians... well, the clients of this restaurant were incredibly wealthy. The menus didn't have prices on it, and you might imagine why not. These people had no financial troubles. They cared nothing about being charged €27 for an egg. I'm sure they paid more in other places. A flacon of vinegar was €200. "What?! Is that liquid gold?" I asked outraged.

"It's twenty years old. The crème de la crème, more valuable than gold."

Bottles of wine of €700 were nothing to them, and the list could go on indefinitely.

One day, however, at lunch time, a group of thirteen people made their way (amid 1 m of snow) in our small restaurant. The owners (a married couple—the chef and head waiter) plus the *sommelier* paid them little attention because they didn't seem affluent enough. For me, they were valuable customers, and I treated them with the same honour I treated the Princess of Qatar. I never made any distinction between wealthy and poor. The only difference I made was between rude and polite humans. And they were very polite and... excited to be there. They came to Cortina on holiday directly from freezing Russia, and that restaurant was on their "to do" list.

I don't want to stereotype, but some people crave to eat in a place that has some stars in a book. They showed me the Michelin guide, and I gathered right away why all that exuberance. It was a dream for them. Anyway, the fact is that none of them spoke any Italian or English and none of the staff knew

Russian. Wow, that day was going to be something to remember. I was assigned to them, of course. I always had the most difficult situations anyway. I was very happy to serve because those people exhilaration was contagious. But how to take a food order from someone you don't understand? I tried speaking in Romanian hoping someone will understand a word. Then Spanish, Italian, English… Nothing at all. They all looked at me with bemusement. I started laughing as their expressions were incredibly funny. They joined me right away, and the restaurant echoed with laughter. I turned around and spotted the staff looking at me with despise. The chef pointed to his watch with impatience which meant, "Stop wasting time. Do your job!"

I tried to transmit to those people (middle-aged and older) something with my hands, monkeys' style. They followed and started to make weird sounds with their mouths. One of them had a Russian – English dictionary, but it was very difficult to use, and it took him ages to find any word. Back then the technology wasn't this advanced, but even it was, Cortina had very poor internet signal. I always wondered how that could be. Such a posh location with unbelievable week mobile coverage and only years after I left Italy I understood why. Cortina was the place for VIPs who wanted privacy!

Anyway, these humorous Russians had no device that could translate anything. Maybe the restaurant should have provided one. The sign and sound languages were the only ones that helped me get their order. In a few minutes various cow, pig, lamb, chicken noises disturbed the soberness of that Michelin restaurant. One wanted fish and pointed me to look at his mouth that resembled a fish breathing under water. Another one put his hands on his head like two horns with meant he fancied venison. A rather elderly women oinked and snorted like a pro. I thought she wanted pork, but when she pointed to a black scarf, I knew she meant wild boar (swine).

The owners were fuming, but we were cracking up. I don't think I ever laughed that much in my entire life. My face, abdomen, and chest were hurting like Hell because of the hilarity of the situation. I was red as a ripe tomato. I should have been more professional, but I really couldn't refrain myself. I guess that whoever watched that scene thought we were all insane. The gloomy owners and the sommelier had no doubt of the truthfulness of that thought. I cared nothing about their opinion. I was doing my job to the best of my abilities. If they had to be the ones to take that order, I'm sure they would have invited them out. And not because they couldn't have reached an agreement but because they despised average customers in general.

Fish, lamb, venison, beef, mostly meet was the food they wanted to eat, and I delivered it with diligence. Finding out which ordered what, was once again very challenging but we teamed up and everybody had what they craved for. When leaving they handed me a 20 EUR banknote which I gave to the head waiter (owner). She took it and threw it with visible disgust in the tips box. I had the time of my life and cared absolutely nothing about the meagre tip. Those people had a dream and fulfilled it paying a huge price. I thought it was more they could afford and felt very grateful.

Yes, they ordered vodka. *Grappa* in Italian but I

had reasons to believe they were quite disappointed. No surprise.

Anyway, the next day while in town, I heard a group of people calling my name. I didn't look because I didn't think I was the chosen person. I didn't know anyone in town. But when someone grabbed my sleeve I had to stop. It was the Russian group. I said, "hello, how are you?" but of course, they understood only the first part. There was no way we could have a normal conversation. Their expression was exhilarant like the day before. Adorable aliens. We looked one at another and cracked up again. Funny signs and noises drew attention to us (again), but we couldn't care less. They were thrilled to see me, and it was evident they wanted to show their gratitude to me for bringing them the food they ordered in a language that most human fail to comprehend. We hugged a few times, the males kissed my hand and we all said goodbye laughing our socks off.

I will always remember them because they were so different from everyone else. So real, happy, and full of life. Humans, the opposite of my employers.

An invaluable drawing

A month or so after Asiago, I ended up in a real Inferno—a hotel on the beach of the Adriatic Sea in Pinarella di Cervia/Ravenna. From a heavy layer of mistreatment that pushed me into darkness, one fascinating occurrence prevents me from washing up from my memory that appalling period. A five-year-old boy's gift. He was a guest at the hotel with his grandparents, and I served them for a week or less.

One day, they waited for me to finish the morning shift and asked if I had a few minutes. I always made time for customers, of course. The timid boy handed me a piece of paper on which he drew two figures holding hands. One was me. "For Cristina," it was written on it. I burst into tears. I didn't think I deserved that affection from anyone. I only did my job with diligence and smiled with kindness to everyone. The child saw in me something I couldn't even imagine because of the inexcusable treatment of my colleagues. Yes, I always had a chat with him and brought him everything he desired, but that was and is me. I do my best in my job, even if my wage is a disgrace or I am treated awfully. I do it because I choose to.

Why only that family noticed?

Anyway, the past is past. I consider that innocent drawing one of the most valuable possessions I've got. I took it home and conserved it in a box amid important documents and pictures. When I'm in need of love, I pull it out and remember the incredibly sweet smile and pure affection of a child who had a

glimpse of my soul.
May the universe be always on his side.

Three weeks a human in Asiago

It was February of 2003. I was driving home from Cortina, a famous posh holiday location in the Dolomites, after five months of work in Hell—a restaurant that doesn't exist nowadays. Thank God for that.

Home meant where my brother was residing, a room in a building attached to the restaurant he was working for. A place where I also slogged for almost two years before going to Cortina. I was supposed to stay for a couple of days until figuring out where to go and what to do next.

You might know that in Italy snows a lot in the mountains. That year was particularly generous with the number of snowflakes. My burgundy car, Ypsilon 10 (Lancia), despite the winter wheels, struggled on the thick layer of sparkling white powder. Luckily, once I left the Dolomites, 70 km more or less farther, the roads were free and easy to drive on. I slowed down and stopped quite a few times to enjoy the majestic scenarios. Wherever you looked, the tall evergreen trees were standing still in the snow making you feel small and fragile. I inhaled the cold pure air and filled the lungs with it. It hurt somehow like it was too much oxygen all at once. In love with Mother Nature, regardless of the physical pain, I admired the stunning views. It was the best feeling I had in a very long time. While I was experiencing this moment of peace and felicity, my mobile rang. I looked at it and didn't recognise the number, but I answered anyway. A woman's voice asked me if I was interested in a temporary waitressing position.

"I'm just going home after resigning from a similar role in Cortina. I'm actually looking for a new job. Where are you located?"

"Perfect timing then. We are in Asiago, Vicenza. When can you be here?"

"I need to get somewhere first, still 90 km to go. I think tomorrow afternoon. When would you need me?" I asked.

"Tomorrow is great. Thank you, Cristina. I know it's short notice, but we've been trying to reach you for a long time. We've got your CV from an employment agency near Pordenone a couple of months back."

"I'm sorry. Cortina lacks phone signals. If you read my resume, you know that this would be my second time in this job. Right? I have only five months of practice."

"It's okay, we need someone just like you. We are waiting for you tomorrow afternoon. Have you ever been to Asiago?" the woman asked.

"No. I heard of Asiago cheese though." Such a cliché.

"Ha, ha, ha. We are indeed famous for a delicious trademark cheese. I hope you are an experienced driver. The roads are icy and quite tricky around here."

"I learnt to drive last year, but I'll be fine."

"Okay. I shall see you tomorrow then. Don't hesitate to call in case you need directions or any help at all."

"See you tomorrow," I said with a mix of excitement and apprehension.

The five months in Cortina had been extremely

challenging, but I absorbed a lot, so I was grateful for the chance they gave me to learn on the job. For most people waiting tables is a low-level occupation, for me was a step up.

I had no idea where Asiago was, but I didn't have time to worry. It was getting dark, and a few glittering snowflakes started to fell from the sky. I love snow with all my heart as it reminds me of my home and the Christmas period.

I looked up, opened my arms, and allowed the cold fluffy snowflakes to touch my face. I had no real place to go, and I was so fatigued. The desire to lay on the snow and stay in that moment forever was ardent but impossible. I sighed, got back in the car, and drove toward the place I thought I would never see again. Luckily, I was about to meet my little brother, so I smiled at the thought and tried to stay positive.

It was dark when I got there. As every Monday, my brother was doing some gardening. We hugged and later in the evening, we told stories. As I mentioned earlier, I was supposed to stay with him for a couple of days, but as that unexpected job came up, I let him know I was going to leave the very next morning. Then we went to bed because I wasn't feeling well. We both thought it was because of the accumulated tiredness.

For those who don't know, when all restaurants and hotels personnel sign a seasonal contract in the mountains or to the sea, it means that they will work for at least sixteen hours a day, for seven days a week. That, of course, depends on the place and manager's or owner's requirement. I am speaking from experience and from what I heard from my colleagues. Some are luckier than others, and many earn a considerable amount of money in that five or six months of intensive work. I knew loads of people who worked one season and lived a decent life for the rest of the year with that income.

As you know (if you read my history), luck avoided me diligently in Italy, so I wasn't among the blessed ones, on the contrary. My bank account was only 1,200 EUR richer than it was four months before. That because I had no experience, stated my employer. The fact I worked harder than everybody else in that restaurant or that I was the person for whom most clients were coming back didn't count at all. Never mind though, this is a happy story.

My brother wasn't used to having guests and sleeping with someone in the same room, so he had very big issues falling asleep. In the morning, I felt that something wasn't quite right, but again, I blamed the weariness and got on my way to a friend where I had all my belongings. After 70 km of driving on hectic roads, I stopped at a traffic light and realised I wasn't able to distinguish the colours on it, thus I didn't know when to move on. The chauffeurs behind honked me with rage so I drove on by inertia utterly confused. I wasn't colour blind, then what was the reason for what just happened? Patience.

I was in town and only a few kilometres away from my friend's workplace. This friend was a man deeply in love with me. However, I never felt anything else but friendship for him. He knew that very well because we've discussed it many times. I got there, parked the car with extreme difficulty as I couldn't see much, went inside and sat on an armchair without saying a word. He looked at me and understood right away it was an emergency. I tried to speak, but I couldn't so he called an ambulance. I was burning hot, my chest was aching, and breathing was a tremendous effort. I can't recall if the ambulance took me to the hospital or it was my friend's doing. I was in a parallel universe, and for the first time in my life, I was hallucinating.

When the doctor asked me to pull up my blouse so he could check my lungs, I started shouting that my lungs were absolutely fine. Yes, this I remember.

"I am not ill. I can't be ill! I am never ill. I need to go to work. I am expected!"

I was probably sedated and fell into a very agitated sleep in which I kept hearing voices saying that my fever was not going down and there was a need for another injection. Someone was cooling my forehead and arms with cold patches. I was shivering from all my muscles. My teeth were grinding and all of a sudden, I started coughing. I was so shocked that I stopped breathing. I never coughed before, maybe when I was a child, but I couldn't remember. I didn't even know how to cough. Everything hurt like I had been hit with a bat thousands of times.

I regained consciousness in the evening and asked for my mobile immediately. My friend was sitting on a chair and said he spoke with Asiago and informed them I was in the hospital.

"How do you know about this?" I asked surprised.

"You shouted quite a few times that you were expected, so I checked your mobile and called them."

"They didn't believe, did they? Only yesterday I conveyed to them. This sounds like a stupid excuse. I really wanted to go there. That woman seemed so nice. Plus, I don't have where to stay. I needed that job."

"Calm down, Cristina. They were actually very understanding and said they will wait until you get better. Anyway, you can stay with me for a few days."

I couldn't believe what I heard. "You live with your parents who can't stand the sight of me. You said it yourself that they don't like Romanians. I should be in Asiago right now!" As I was saying that the doctor got in to speak to me.

"Welcome back, Miss G., we almost lost you there. What was in your head to drive for nearly 80 km with 41°C fever? You have bronchitis, did you know that?"

I thought it was a joke and started laughing. One of my sisters is a nurse, she practised on me when I was a child. Every time she came home and studied, asked me to interrogate her. Children memorise almost everything they hear, so I knew quite a lot about medicine and diseases. I couldn't have bronchitis. I never coughed, had pain in my chest but most importantly, I wasn't a smoker. I have been feeling unwell for the last two months, but only because I was exhausted. The doctor blamed the high fever for my behaviour, but when I realised he was not smiling, the news hit me with astronomical power.

"But I'm a waitress, I work with food and people! Bronchitis is highly contagious! Oh, God," I cried out loud. The doctor said nothing and waited for me to calm down. I thought for a while and dared to doubt of the analyses' results.

"I came to Italy almost three years ago and had a complete check-up. They looked into all my medical history from Romania, vaccines, hospitalisations, etc., and found nothing wrong with me. I had a chest Xray, breasts, gynaecological, eyes control. It all came up clean. They told me I was as healthy as a horse (the man I was supposed to marry asked for this health examination. You know if you read my Italian story)."

"It's not that old," said the doctor.

"But I don't cough!"

"You do now."

"Can I keep being a waitress? I was intended to go to work in a hotel in Asiago. I'm expected there. I'm a reliable person, I can't call and come with another excuse. I'm striving to build a career. I need to go now!"

"You can work among people as long as you don't cough in their faces and keep a very high level of hygiene. However, you should rest for at least two weeks. You have a gaunt figure, and it's obvious you're exhausted. I don't think you could keep up with any employment right now, especially not with waitressing. It's too demanding."

I smiled and thought he didn't know how determined and strong I was. "I don't have the luxury of resting or falling apart. Can I go now?" I asked.

The doctor signed the discharge papers, gave me several antibiotic prescriptions, and said it was up to me what to do next. "You are putting your life at stake though."

I thanked him and went with my friend. I needed to buy antibiotics right away, so we searched for a pharmacy opened at that hour in the night. It wasn't an easy task, but we found one and bought everything I needed: syrups, paracetamol, and the pills that were supposed to cure my chest infection.

At home, his livid parents were expecting us. I felt

very bad for them. I didn't want to be there, but I had nowhere else to go. I didn't call my brother because that room wasn't his place. He had no power of decision anyway.

The next day I called the hotel apologising in every way I could. "I'm truly mortified. This is the first time in my life I'm so poorly. I have never, ever been to a doctor because of an illness before. I wish I were there now, I promise."

"We know, Cristina. Your friend called and explained everything. He was afraid you were going to die, to be honest. Well, maybe you could join our team next year?"

"No, no. I'll come as soon as my fever goes back to normal. I'm taking antibiotics and had a few shots in the hospital. I'm sure that I'll be able to drive tomorrow afternoon. Do you think you can wait until then?"

"That doesn't sound like a good idea, but you know better. The person you are supposed to replace agreed to remain until Friday night. If you think you can be there before that, then we'll wait."

It was probably Wednesday when I talked to them. If my memory doesn't play tricks on me, I stayed in bed for two days—never living the room as I couldn't face those people. Especially because my friend was at work during the day. When he came home, I told him I was going to leave the next day if he gave me a lift to pick up my car and a few things from the storeroom where he put my belongings (his workplace was a shop with a large basement deposit).

"Are you out of your mind? You almost kicked the bucket! You are too weak. You must have lost like 10 kg since I last saw you. Do you realise you weight maybe 40 kg now? That's why you got ill. You need to rest, you heard the doctor."

No, I didn't know I lost weight. I had been too busy and focused on learning the job, oblivious to everything else. "I can't stay here, and I need this," I said.

We left the next day very early in the morning. My cough was bad, really bad. When it started, I had to sit, grab on something, or lean against a wall to avoid falling on the floor. Fortunately, I always felt it coming and had plenty of time to act accordingly and preclude airborne contamination. I carried with me packs of tissues and quite a few bottles of disinfectant. My chest hurt and burnt like Hell, and I had troubles breathing. My body temperature was still around 39°C, but I knew it was just a matter of time until it went back to normal. The antibiotics always worked miracles.

I stayed in the shop until after midday to make sure my sight was all right. I was determined to drive 100 km but didn't want to jeopardise the life of other people. When the fever reached 38 °C, I took my car and drove to Asiago. I stopped a few times when sudden cough attacks knocked me down and got there four hours later. It normally takes two hours. However, the road was terrible. I believe I counted nine extremely dangerous uphill hairpins. Perfect for motorcyclists, but definitely not fun for someone in my situation. Only then I realised why the question regarding my experience as a driver. I had little. Cortina's roads were quite knotty, but nothing compared to those hairpins. Anyway, I loved driving back then.

***

Asiago, the main centre of the largest Plateau in Italy, isn't famous only for its DOP (AOC in English) cheese as I used to think. Situated in the Prealps—at 1,001 m above sea level—the town is a perfect location for skiing and hiking, like Cortina. But if Cortina is a posh locality appreciated by national and international celebrities, head of states—and many other VIPs—mostly very wealthy people, Asiago is favourite by regular families who like peace and tranquillity. The gorgeous little town is a gem of architecture with bright streets, huge squares, and breathtaking panoramas. Mother Nature has been very generous with this touristic site. If you ever visit Italy and find yourself in Veneto—near Vicenza—don't hesitate to visit it. Especially if you're fond of hiking and uncontaminated nature.

***

It was dark when I parked the car and got in the hotel where everybody was waiting for me. The warmth received from the managing director, receptionists and all the staff overwhelmed me. I have never felt that welcomed anywhere in my life until then. It was truly touching. During the journey, I worried about the fact that they thought my hasty illness was just an excuse. In the car, I disinfected my hands and face thoroughly. Inside, I did my best not to cough or exhale in humans' faces.

I didn't tell them my illness was contagious. The doctor gave me free will and told me to be careful. I had a work permit that stated I was fit to be in the midst of people. All workforces that came in direct contact with food had to have one. It was the law. You couldn't get a job without it, not legally at least.

I should have said something about my temporary

health situation, but I wanted the job too much. In the end, it was going to be only for three weeks. They didn't ask because there wasn't time for an investigation. The person who had to leave needed an immediate replacement. It was my fault they didn't look for another person, I held them back. Then again, they didn't enquire because no sane person would go to work if they were very ill, right? They didn't even imagine the severity of my situation. Smiling with all my teeth, I said it was an old flu that reached the peak the other day, but I was better and ready for work.

They congratulated my incredible capacity for recovery, checked both my work and residency permit and I signed a short-term contract. That evening I had my first shift in a hotel because I asked for it. Wow! What a massive difference between the average restaurant in Cortina and that four-stars place.

I coughed, of course. That bad that I had to lean against a wall far from food and people. All my colleagues came to the rescue. The chef himself abandoned the pans and ran toward me. Red like a ripe tomato, I solicited them to stay away. "It's just a cough. The physical support is because I'm weak. Nothing to worry about. Please, give me some space."

They did as I asked and thought I was utterly insane to have agreed to work in those conditions. You could tell that all cared for real. It brought tears to my eyes. I thought I was dreaming or maybe hallucinating. I smiled and thanked them dearly, then went to the restroom, washed my hands and face with soap and ran into the restaurant to do my job.

The hotel was a favourite by families. Almost every table had children. I played with them in between meals. I brought them everything they asked with diligence and joy. My chest hurt and every muscle in my body screamed in pain, but my face was radiant. I absolutely loved everything in that place. It had a very positive vibration, and I resonated with it.

Three attacks of cough made me interrupt the *service* (as we call it) for a few minutes that evening. But other than that, everything went all. I smiled with all my teeth and walked quite a few kilometres, I think. The place was enormous.

When the customers left the restaurant, all the staff teamed up to prepare the room for breakfast. We emptied the tables, changed the cloths, hoovered, washed and dried up the glasses. The manager director came to check I was okay. He was informed about my coughing. I assured him that there was absolutely nothing wrong with me. "Why? Have I disappointed you? Has someone complained about me?" I asked with worry.

"On the contrary. You are a breath of fresh air in this hotel. Except for the *maître* and a couple of waiters, all the other staff is local. They've known one another for years. You are an exotic appearance. Every client you served was fascinated by you, so are your colleagues."

Incredulous but happy, I blushed tremendously. I really didn't think I was all that breath of fresh air, but I certainly did my best. But not only that evening, all my life I strived to give my best in everything. However, those people were the only ones who noted and appreciated it.

I had been given a bed in a shared room, but my roommate was the person I came to replace, so she left that evening. I preferred to sleep alone in a room and couldn't believe my good fortune. My feet were swollen, and I could barely walk, but I showed no sign of pain. When my colleagues accompanied me to my room, they said they were going out and invited me to join them. I thought I was going to die if I made another step, but I couldn't refuse. I *didn't want* to refuse. They seemed so amazing, so fun, and so human. Besides, it was only 10 pm. Way too early for a waiter to go to bed. It's true that I signed up for the next morning shift that started at seven, but they didn't know that.

I had a shower, dressed up, and went with them to a dancing club. I sat the whole time but didn't say why. I felt that my feet had an issue I wasn't used to, but I didn't know what it was. We joked, laughed, paid compliments one to another, and it was a wonderful evening. The first one since I was in Italy.

When back, I slept like a baby for a couple of hours. At 6 am, my alarm went off. I jumped to my feet, and an excruciating pain knocked me down. My legs refused to follow my instructions. I checked my feet and understood it was serious. However, I was expected downstairs in about twenty-five minutes. I crawled to the bathroom and immersed my feet in cold water for five minutes. I was freezing, but there was no time to feel ill. When the swollenness retreated, and I could stand again, I had a quick shower, put my uniform on, and ran downstairs.

I got there first, then the team leader showed up. In twenty minutes, both of us prepared a huge table with a vast assortment of fruits, vegetables, cheese, jams, croissants, bread, cereals, yoghurts, drinks, and so on. Continental breakfast for every taste and desire. The smell of fresh coffee made me crave for one, but I was too shy to ask. The head waiter, a middle-aged local woman, made a couple and offered me a double espresso.

"You are free to eat and drink everything you desire, just not in front of the guests, of course. Please, we don't want our employee to starve."

A completely different treatment than anywhere else before. All the other employers cared nothing about your hunger or longing. I thanked her with all my heart and sipped the espresso while eating a croissant. I am very fond of coffee, espresso in particular.

Then the guests showed up, and the work began. At 7:30 am another waiter joined to give us a hand. For two and a half hours, we made cappuccinos, served loads of coffee and a few teas, replaced everything that was missing and laughed with the customers. I coughed a few times, but nobody spotted me as I hid in the bathroom. When everyone left, we cleaned the room and sat down to have a discussion. "Cristina. I noticed you are slightly limping. Have you hurt your legs or feet?" asked my superior.

I was shocked as I had no idea of limping at all. "No, I had no trauma to my legs or feet, however, since last evening they got swollen, and the pain is considerable. I really don't know why. I never had this issue before."

"Let me see your shoes," she asked.

I found that request bizarre, but I bent and took off one of my black flat shoes and gave it to her.

She took it in her hands and said they were quality shoes and seemed comfortable. "Have you ever worked on a carpeted floor as a waitress?"

"No. This is the second place where I wait tables. The other one had wooden floor, and my feet were fine."

"Then it must be the carpet. You are not the only one to face this problem. In fact, some people had to resign because of it. I too suffer from time to time. Do you have another pair of shoes? With a leather sole perhaps? The ones you're wearing now have a plastic one. From my experience, the leather helps a lot."

Luckily, I had exactly what she suggested. The second pair of flat shoes were extremely expensive and avoided wearing them daily. However, if that was the solution to my sore feet, then I was more than happy to put them *to dance*. That was the reason I bought them anyway.

The boss gave me some arnica cream to spread on my feet and sent me to rest for an hour until the next shift. But before I left I asked her if I could do all the three shifts every day for those weeks. She said it was too hard to keep up with so many hours, but because all my colleagues were tired after a few months of intensive work, she was happy to sign me up for as many shifts I could and wanted to take.

"Even if at the very last moment to replace someone or help in the kitchen. I really need the hours and to practise more with experienced staff like this."

She took act of my desire to learn and serve and praised me dearly.

I had been sleeping with my feet on a pillow since I moved to Italy, so I kept doing it. They got better after the cream and the change of shoes, but the swelling was stubborn. However, I didn't complain once. What was the point? I kept coughing suddenly and terribly, but always far from people and food—rigorously leant against a wall. I took my antibiotics every four hours daily and ameliorated by the minute.

Every day went the same way. I woke up at 6:00 or 6:30 am, served breakfast, polished glasses, cleaned the room for lunch then went to rest for an hour or so. Around 11:30 am, all the staff had a meal together, then served lunch to the guests, cleaned the room and prepared it for dinner. At 5:45 pm, whoever wanted had a quick tea (even those who were not expected to work the evening shift), then ensured dinner service to customers. Then again, cleaned the room, hoovered, polished glasses, cutlery, and made everything ready for the next meal service. All these duties were always divided and assigned by the head waiter following a specific pattern. She made sure that every each of us had a different task, so we don't feel bothered or annoyed. Most of my colleagues disliked hoovering because the room was huge and it took a lot of time, so I always offered to exchange my assigned task, but we needed our superior permission to do whatever we pleased. At first, she said it was unfair and urged us to keep up with our responsibilities, but when I explained that I was more than happy with doing that, she gave her authorisation. Then she had another private discussion with me.

"Why do you always offer to do the hardest chores when most people run from?" she asked confused.

"Because a job is a job and we signed a contract knowing what is expected of us. You can't pick and choose. Someone has to do it. I learnt this as a child. It's my nature, nothing is too hard for me. Seriously, I am not bothered. If you're having issues with finding someone to do something, ask me. If I know how to do it, I'll do it, if not, teach me."

She was very impressed and showed it often.

Some afternoons, before dinner, the staff gathered in a room downstairs to tell funny stories. Two evenings a week, mostly Fridays and Saturdays, we went wandering in the quirky town or had a drink in a bar. We bond the very first day. The manager was right, I was an alien that everybody liked. The cooks always asked me if I fancied something special to eat. The people in charge with the storeroom filled with jams, sweets, cheese, offered me every day something sweet to take in my room after my shift. "You are so thin and poorly, please have this."

I was astonished by their disinterested care and kindness. There was a girl who didn't like me much though. She made no secret of it. My lipstick was too red for her taste, my eyes too grey, my shirts too white, and my tights were way too expensive for a job like ours. I told her I was sorry my presence made her unhappy. The head waiter kept her at a distance, in fact, she was often given a free day. Then I realised why she was so upset with me. I took her hours. I spoke with my superior, and she told me it wasn't my fault. "She brought this on herself. She's very abrupt with customers, she almost never smiles and her tights are often broken. She doesn't look or strive to be professional. In fact, this is the last season this girl will be working with us. The manager took pity of her because there isn't much to do in this little town, but she's too stubborn and doesn't want to follow the rules. We had loads of complaints. Too much of a disappointment. So, please don't feel guilty if she doesn't get a shift. You have nothing to do with it."

I felt sorry for her nevertheless. Asiago is a picturesque town in the Prealps, very valued by many people around the world, but too little for a young girl. The astonishing landscape in winter time, during the whole year actually, took the breath away to any tourist, but it looked trivial to her. The girl confessed to me more than once that she didn't like living there. I understood her very well and said the world is huge. She just needed to pack a bag and leave. Maybe she listened, I don't know.

***

One day, most likely a Sunday, in the corner of the restaurant an elderly man was sitting alone at a table and looked toward the huge room. The manager came and solicited me to take his table although it wasn't on my side. I didn't query why that odd request, I did what required. After bringing him lunch, the old man asked me several questions. It was clear he liked talking. It was a glorious day in the mountains, most of the guests were skiing on a perfect snow. It wasn't much to do in the restaurant, so I stopped and answered all the queries he rose. Conveying with customers is in a waitress's duties anyway. The man was really kind and full of compliments.

After he had left, the managing director told me he was the owner of the hotel and came that Sunday to meet me as he heard a lot about my exoticism. I felt incredibly privileged and spoiled.

***

A week after I got there, two of the families with loads of children I served, left the hotel and all came to say goodbye. I wasn't used to it. At Cortina, the

195

place I worked in was a restaurant. People came and went the same day. But here, I saw those people twice a day (or more often) for more than a week. We laughed, joked, and bonded a lot. Everybody was calling me by name and children grabbed my hand every time I walked by their table. I was really sorry to see them leaving.

After giving me a quick hug, the head of one family reached a hand out to me and expressed gratitude for my professionalism. I reached my right hand by instinct, and he put a 20 EUR banknote in it. Caught by surprise, I didn't know what to say. It was the very first tip I held in my hands. At Cortina, all the tips were collected by the owner and divided among the staff. Here, the restaurant staff was instructed to keep the tip without being required to let anyone know. However, I went to my superior and told her about it. She reiterated that the money was mine.

I know that for you or anyone that bill was small, but I cared nothing about tips. Not then, not after, not now. I love money, don't get me wrong, I wish I'd have a tip every five minutes, however, my priority was and is for people to be happy with my service. The man who gave me that bill had a large family. I believed it was quite a sacrifice for them and I felt immensely grateful. I got tips of 1,000 EUR after that (divided among the staff), but they meant nothing to me as I heard no *thank you* from those extremely wealthy Qatar people.

***

One Saturday, the hotel gave a party with live music. I can't remember what the occasion was. Three handsome men, a band, brought several instruments.

They rehearsed a few songs to make sure the audio system was okay. I was preparing the room for the banquet. All my other colleagues were resting. One of them asked me at the microphone if I had a favourite song I would like to hear during the party. I blushed surprised and looked down without replying. The boy reiterated the question when the manager got in.

"Cristina," he said, "the man wants to sing for you. You must have a song you like. Tell them."

I walked to the singer and said I loved *"Margherita"* by Riccardo Cocciante.

"Oh, we never sang it, and I don't know it. I'm sorry," he said.

I found it very strange they didn't know a classic, but hey, I knew nothing about live bands. He asked me if I had a different song. Unfortunately, that was the only one I knew.

I finished to prepare the room and went to have a shower and get changed. The party was lovely, people had so much fun. They sang, danced, and played games. We served food and smiled at everyone. Suddenly, the singer said, "To Cristina" and started singing, *"Margherita."* What a surprise! My eyes blurred with tears.

When the party was over, the girl I was no friends with, another local girl who helped with the busy shift and I were cleaning the room. The singer asked in the microphone if we wanted to go for a drink in town. The girls agreed with joy, I was very reticent. There was something odd on that invitation, at least that was my perception. Although I was twenty-eight, my naivety was quite thick. When the girls went out, I asked him if there was a hidden intention in that request. He laughed and gave me a negative answer.

But I wasn't convinced, so I went to one of my male colleagues to seek advice. He told me it was most certainly a very explicit not so candid invitation. I wasn't shocked or disappointed, just slightly sad. I went back, finished the shift, and prepared to go to my room. My feet were still quite sore, as every day and I really didn't feel like wasting time with men who looked for free sex. The girls and the other tow boys from the band agreed to meet outside in ten minutes. I reiterated my question to the singer as I really liked him (especially because he sang my song for me), highlighting the fact that I had no intention of having sex with him.

"I am happy to have a drink with you, but if this is a sex request, then don't come knocking on my door because I am not interested." He denied laughing. Again. I went to my room, had a shower and went to bed alone, falling asleep in a heartbeat. I don't know if he knocked on my door or not, the girls never spoke about it. My guess is that he didn't.

It was a normal life for everybody except me, and I didn't hold a grudge. My co-workers used to say, "whatever we do during the season remains here." I thought it was a diabolic pact but never discussed it. It was not my business. Nobody is perfect and who can actually tell for sure what's normal and what's not? Despite not being a part of their world, those people cared for me in a very unbiased way. All I could feel was endless gratitude.

When the season was over, and the hotel didn't need so much personnel, my time in Heaven came to an end. I really didn't want to go. I became friends with everyone in there (except the bored girl). The town was incredibly beautiful with quirky shops and smiling people. It was Paradise for me. But I had to say goodbye. I was the last one to leave out of the seasonal workers, and I cried when the other went on their way.

The maître offered me a job in a hotel in Padova-Terme where he was head of staff. I refused although I'm not sure why. Maybe because it was supposed to start in May and I needed a job and a place to stay right then. He gave me his business card and told me to call him anytime if I changed my mind. "You might not have a lot of experience, but you have a gift, Cristina. Clients like you instantly. I don't know if it's your red lipstick, the smile, the yearn to please them, your aura, or all together, but you are born to work with people. You have a very bright future in this business. You'll become a professional in no time. You are one of the most proficient waitresses I've ever had the fortune to work with. Please, think about it. I could help you."

I felt flattered because I didn't feel I was good enough for a place like the one he told me about. I was, of course, aware of the fact that the customers appreciated me. Many preferred me instead of the highly trained personnel because my passion and desire to always do the best was natural and very conspicuous. Everyone noticed I loved that job.

When the manager called me into his office for getting paid, he praised my work dearly. I must admit that I had a terrible crush on that man. Sadly for me, he got married the year before. But there was a rumour going around that he felt the same for me. Yes, I sensed it, and that day I had the proof which I choose to keep for myself. However, he never, ever made me feel uncomfortable, and we never talked about it. He was a devoted husband and a perfect boss.

After a small chit-chat, he handed me a check of 800,00 EUR. I couldn't believe my eyes. Despite the fact that I worked three shifts almost every day, I don't think I accumulated more than eight hours a day. While in Cortina, I worked for at least sixteen hours (often more) nearly every day, and they paid me 1,200 EUR for four months!

"This is too much," I exclaimed. "I am still in training," so to speak.

"On the contrary. You did a great job and deserve this and more. I hope we'll see you again, possibly next season, if you want."

Of course I wanted, I couldn't wait. He hugged me tightly, and I left after saying goodbye to everyone. I cried for all the journey also because my future was terribly uncertain. I stopped quite a few times to admire the views and to memorise everything I could. The cough was still present, although seldom. The feet were sore, but my heart was filled with love and gratitude for those incredible (almost) three weeks in Heaven among angels.

Never in my life I've encountered such amazing folks like in Asiago. After that, you know what happened. I kept hoping to meet other people like them, but my vibration wasn't right.

Why were those humans so remarkably distinct, I can't really tell. They were all Italians, and I was still Romanian.

What was the difference between the Asiago, Cortina and all the other people I came across after that?

Only the universe can give an answer. I am still

waiting for it.

***

A month after I left, I received another check of 1,000 EUR from them. I had to call and ask if it was a mistake. They said it wasn't. That was the right pay of a waiter in a busy period in a place that respected people and adhered the law. On no occasion I worked for another honest company like that. They paid me for every minute I worked and charged me for nothing. I ate, slept, washed my clothes in there. Moreover, I was spoiled by everyone, and they rewarded me for everything.

Unfortunately, I never went back or heard from them again. Things happened, my situation precipitated terribly after that and it went from bad to worse. I moved to Perugia and lost contact with them.

To the day, when people treat me wrong, I think of Asiago and hold on to that priceless memory. Those people are the proof that humanity still coexists in humans and I will always have faith in mankind.

I have a tremendous wish to mention the name of the hotel because it deserves a lot of public and official recognition, but the fact I was hired with a chest infection might have negative consequences on it. I am gutted, but the law is law. They didn't know, I kept it a secret. My work permit was legitimate, signed by a doctor after a thorough medical examination. It held no restrictions, on the contrary, it stated clearly that I was healthy and fit to work amidst people. To the day, the staff of that extraordinary hotel is oblivious of the serious illness I was affected by.

But if you go to Asiago and need accommodation,

drop me a line, and I will reveal in private to you the name of Paradiso. It's a four-star hotel, with a huge wellness centre, immersed in a perfect green or an immaculate white, depending on the season. If you like skiing, hiking, stunning panoramas, *beautiful* food (especially cheese), it's the right place for you and your family. Spending the Christmas in there is a magical dream that will come true one day.

Bloody spaghetti!

This is another humorous story (now, not then) from which I learnt that humans can adapt to absolutely everything if they have will and patience.

The second day I got to Italy, I was taken to visit Rome for the Great Jubilee in 2000. In there I walked on my knees for 1 Km or so. So painful! I hope God forgave at least ten of my capital sins. No, not from my own initiative, no, no. I wasn't so eager to ruin my delicate knees. I was expected to do so as my companions were a nun and a priest. Never again I swore.

Then we went and stopped for a night in *Casa del Pellegrino*—a religious Sanctuary in Collevalenza/Perugia—for another celebration. Two Romanian sisters were to take their oaths. Again, it wasn't from my own desire. I didn't even know those people! A feast took place, and we were served *maltagliati al pomodoro* which is a sort of homemade pasta terribly wrong cut—it's supposed to be this way (irregular shapes), a real treat—with tomato sauce. After endless hours in a car (probably more than twelve), the kilometres on my knees (one, I know, but it seemed more like ten. You try it and let me know,) the various religious services and celebrations, I was utterly famished.

Romania didn't have pasta in its cuisine back then. Nowadays it's a classic. That was a first for me. It didn't look good, I am telling you. That red sauce on unsystematic pieces of flat pasta seemed like a dish that came directly from a battlefield. It's a too sanguine analogy, I know, but that's exactly what I thought. My childhood revulsion toward the tomato sauce shrouded my entire being. I stared at the plate and felt no tempting desire to try it. My stomach was making noises, but I wasn't brave enough. My tablemates started talking to me in Italian, asking why wasn't I eating. Man, I have never spoken Italian except for the first dinner to an Italian family. I mean, I really couldn't explain myself clearly. I understood everything they said, but couldn't reply. When I did try it at the insistence of everyone around me, my whole body screamed in horror. Absolutely revolting. Never in my life, I tasted something more disgusting. That moment I knew,' Italy's favourite and the most common food is pasta. I am going to die of undernourished in one of the most famous countries for its gastronomy, among many other things.'

I probably ate the desert and some fruits, but I was still terribly hungry. The next day before leaving, they served us lunch. 'Please, please, not *pasta al pomodoro*!' The universe must have been busy with important stuff for this time, were spaghetti with tomato sauce. That made me think that the chef wasn't aware of the existence of other sauces like carbonara, amatriciana, bolognese, puttanesca, and so on. I felt like crying, and my stomach hurt so I imposed myself to try it. I was going to remain in that country for an indefinite time, I had to learn to like the food to avoid inanition.

Do you believe that?

How can anyone starve in Italy? They have one of the most spectacular food cultures in the whole world! It was outrageous what I thought and felt terribly guilty. I prayed God to give me strength and courage like I was about to poison myself and most certainly die or twist in agony. I took the fork, sighed a few times, and attempted to eat some bloody (literally) spaghetti. Ha! What arrogance! They all fell with a seismic splash on my plate. I, with the fork still up in the air and my mouth wide open, stopped breathing. You should have seen my tablemates faces and their clothes. Covered in red sauce. The table cloth too, glasses, bottles... A disaster I could have never imagined. What the heck?! They were spaghetti, not bombs! It wasn't funny at all. I was flabbergasted and wished to hide into a hole and never get out. A few sisters ran to our table and helped the guests, all priests wearing white robes on top of the black ones, to clean themselves. God only knows why they had those white robes on at that time of the day—to lunch with a clumsy Romanian! Really?! I mean, it wasn't on purpose, was it?! A sort of diabolic prank?

I was mortified. My face was most certainly red before it happened, but at that point, I felt like my eyes were on fire. My hair, my ears, every part of my body was burning. When I restarted breathing, I was inhaling and exhaling the flames of Hell.

I don't know what happened after that, but the priest—our driver—was a joker. I'm sure he made fun of me during the whole trip back, 500 km. It wasn't the first time. He missed no opportunity to laugh on my behalf—a farmer's daughter who never saw more than two villages and four cities in her country. I was his favourite prey. I still have nightmares for all the hoaxes he played on me. Buffoon!

Anyway, a few months later, after I lost 8 or 9 kg, I became addictive to pasta with tomato sauce. When I moved alone, I used to wake up in the middle of the night and make spaghetti al pomodoro (rigorously *al dente*). And I wondered what was in my mind when I predicted death from starvation because the pasta was disgusting. Seriously? It's the most scrumptious food ever! Cheap, easy and fast to cook, versatile—it can be sweet, salty, creamy, cold, hot, carbonised (if you forget it in the oven and go to work), and so on. How could someone *not* love pasta? What's not to like? Especially if it's cooked by me. No false modesty, but I make an excellent tomato sauce. I learnt from the best chef in Italy.

I also became an expert in eating spaghetti like a queen. It's one of the achievements I am most proud of. Working in restaurants has many advantages. Now, even if I want, I can't create a tsunami of sauce on my plate. "Practice makes perfect."

***

If you wonder if there were other facetious stories I could have shared, I am telling you that aren't many, no. Maybe the following deserve mention.

In Cortina, I was confused with a big Italian celebrity and had to run away from a bunch of Japanese girls for I was late to work.

*

In Livigno, I tried to learn skiing and flew like an eagle amid terrified skiers. I could not lean into a turn to create an edge at all. My body slipped on snow like a rocket propelled into the sky, with no curving whatsoever. After fifteen minutes of intensive training (watch *Edie the Eagle*), my instructor (a friend) was truly impressed with my fast learning skills and utter insanity, so he decided it was time to move to a more adequate slope for such a natural talent like me. On my first attempt, I landed on my back with a deafening bang. I was sure that my brain was scattered all over the ski slope. One of my sticks stabbed my right arm. Man, it hurt so badly. I lay on the snow afraid of moving until my instructor came to the rescue. I really didn't want to leave behind my grey matter, so it took him quite some time to convince me that my head was in one piece.

"I don't believe you. I heard a crash, and it hurts like hell. I'm telling you, it's shattered," I mumbled. Once again, I came out of it okay but never touched the skis again. No, no. It's a perilous sport for me, but mostly, for those around me.

*

In my first year of residency in Italy, I went to a shop, and in a very rusty, but serious Italian, I asked for a *penis* holder instead of a *pen* holder. The retailers cracked up. I saw no problem with my pronunciation. I only missed an "n" (*porta pene* instead of *porta penne*).

*

I once stumbled upon something and rolled down from the top of the stairs of a hotel. I reached the end of it laughing my socks off while the staff was staring at me petrified. It all happened in a flash, nobody had time to intervene. My bones remained miraculously intact, but my skin flaunted fifty shades of purple for a few months. Ha, ha. You wish!

***

These were the stories that made me smile during my permanence in Italy. I hope you enjoyed them as much as I did and understood why weren't included in my memoir.

God save the pasta al pomodoro!

Questions raised by You

Some people told me about a money inconsistency in my story. It's unclear how I got a car when I said I was penniless.

I never asserted such a thing. It's true that I went home indigent though, but that's a different story. My statement was that I could barely pay the bills which included the car payments. The first two years after I started working, I saved a considerable amount of money that was spent when I got ill. Buying a second-hand car wasn't that expensive. The insurance was worse because I got my driving licence after the age of twenty-six.

I had three cars while I lived in Italy. The first one was a Fiat Uno (*bianca*/white). If you're Italian, you are aware of the reprehensible fame of that car. I had no idea until after I bought it. Criminal organisation or not, I never liked that car, but a bargain is a bargain. My notorious Fiat Uno was destroyed in an accident only a couple of weeks later. I can't say more because it's a harrowing memory. The second—a burgundy Ypsilon 10—broke down after four or five years of very intensive driving. I was forced to buy another—a sky-blue Grande Punto—for I was living in a small village quite far from my workplace. Italy doesn't have a great public transportation system. On the contrary. But mostly, I needed the car to go to doctors in remote locations.

However, the reason I decided to take the driving licence and buy a car was the sea. That was a year after I left the man who was supposed to become my husband, quite a few years before finding out I was ill.

I have never seen a beach before Italy. Having a walk on the beach was a dream I never dreamed of dreaming. A client of the restaurant I worked for as a dishwasher, offered to take me to the sea one day. I can't remember the reason she decided to do such a charitable act. I'm sure we were never friends, and she wasn't known for having a good heart. Anyway, a Monday morning she came with her daughter and took me to Bibione, a sea location in Veneto/Northeast Italy (between Venezia and Trieste). It was a gorgeous sunny day when we've got there. Although I saw the Lignano beach (a few kilometres away of Bibione) during the ten days I was a babysitter, I couldn't enjoy it or even feel anything positive about it. When I saw Bibione, the blue water, the long golden beaches, I fell irremediably in love. While laying on the sand, I imagined being there at 4 in the morning, utterly alone with the sea. I pictured myself walking up and down, listening to the murmurs of the water and the crashing waves. I fancied filling my lungs with the salty breeze and sleep on the cold sand covered by a warm blanket.

That moment I promised I will go to school and take the driving licence no matter what. The very next day I went and signed up for a driving course. For six months I learnt rules I didn't know existed. Never in my life, I thought I will have a car because back then, Romanian women didn't have the mentality for such a thing. Nowadays it's a must as in every other country.

***

Another confusion (I've been told) is around the fact that I mentioned having a diploma in woodworking but never explained how and when I got it.

This is a slightly different story because it didn't happen in Italy but in Romania. A very sensitive matter I don't enjoy talking about.

When the Communism fell, in December of 1989 (read Oranges at Christmas in a Communist Country), I was fourteen. In the summer of the following year, I was supposed to choose a high-level education school. However, that year the country was in total chaos and most schools closed down. For financial and pragmatic reasons, I decided on a college— Foundation Degree in English—*Professional School* in my country. It lasted for four years in which I studied the same subjects as a bachelor's degree student— Math, Biology, Chemistry, Literature, History, and so on—plus a skill for life which was (is) carpenter with all its academic subjects. I have, therefore, a diploma in woodworking. I can make doors and various pieces of furniture. Essentially, I should know how to build anything from wood. Except I don't. I never liked it, and it's one of the most delicate subjects of discussion for me. My dream was to go to University and become a Psychologist. It took me more than fifteen years to accept that I don't even have a bachelor degree despite loving school with all my heart.

My peer group of students is referred to as *The Generation of Sacrifice* because of the total disarray in which my country plunged after the Communism. Ceausescu was obsessed with the level of culture and knowledge of his people. "Study, study, and study again!" was his favourite slogan (borrowed from Lenin). The education was very severe in the many high schools in usage in his time. When I had to take the most important decision of my life, there weren't many choices. Most of us went *wherever* just to continue the studies. Between becoming a farmer and a carpenter, I had to pick the second one for it involved dealing with books—my greatest passion.

My age group and maybe another one after (I'm not sure), were the only ones who had the luck (or misfortune) to have access to that odd instruction level. A *Professional School* normally has three years, not four—Skills for life equal. A bachelor degree required four years to get it (back then, now it's got five). The huge difference between these two degrees was that the bachelor one allowed you to follow a university right away, but the professional one was not enough. So the generations that chose that type of education wasted four years of their lives and completely destroyed their future. Of course we didn't know that, and maybe we wouldn't have cared much.

If you think that I am too dramatic then read my first memoir about the communist regime.

You are right, one might have followed another school after that and gain control over their future. True, if they had the means. Most hadn't. I am one of them. My weakest subject of discussion.

So here is why I said that I was the only qualified worker in the wood factory where my despicable team leader broke my thumb.

***

Somebody asked how old was the man I was supposed to marry, the one who chose to sleep in his mother's bed rather than in a free bedroom.

I can't believe I've omitted this information! I am truly sorry. The man was thirty-eight at that time. I was twenty-five. This will be developed in a realistic novel soon. Stay tuned!

***

A person I don't know, sent me a private email to ask me how my health is these days keeping in mind I gave up going to doctors. This enquiry brought tears to my eyes. I was deeply touched.

I take loads of painkillers on random days, and I'm grateful for the fact I don't have to go to a pharmacy to buy them, any shop sells them in England. Hurray! But other than that I am doing okay. Much better than I used to when being a patient to cruel doctors. Of course, I don't know what stage is my disease now, but as my life isn't in danger, I don't really care. The other disease is maybe cured despite the fact they told me there was no remedy.

Never give up hope, never stop believing you'll get better! Miracles happen every day.

***

A rather abrupt reader asked what I was aiming at when I wrote *Ten Years in Italy, Three Weeks a Human.*

It has been therapeutic for me, and I believe it's a great story that will make some wonder if it's fair discriminating an entire nation for the mishaps of a few. I didn't write it to attract sympathy or compassion. It has no absolute use to me. The past is gone. I'm not upset anymore. As I said, I am grateful if something. Italian is the most beautiful language in the world, and I can't be prouder for speaking it. When I listen "O Sole mio" I fly in Heaven.

***

If you have any other queries, please visit my blog While I breathe, I hope, or my Facebook page and send me an email.

Thank you, amazing human being, for getting to the end of this little addition to my Italian story.

May the universe be always on your side.

Excerpt from It's Never Game Over

It's over when you die

If change was easy, everybody would do it. – I heard this from several people who made it.

As you might have realised, all the chapters treated one thing only: humans are all the same, what differentiates them is ONE single decision: to fight or to surrender. To strive to change, or to accept what happens to you.

What surprises me the most is the fact that we all want a better life, without doing the work. I wanted that too. For 40 years of my existence, I was a spectator in my life. And I cried when things went from bad to worse. I crawled and bowed my head while I was telling myself that it's going to be sunny on my road too, one day. I thought it will happen because I was a good person. The truth is that we are all good until we take the decision not to be good anymore. And this might happen at any time in our existences. It could occur when we are just a baby. It could happen with or without our knowledge.

I knew I had to change for more than 15 years. If you reach thirty and you feel like you never lived, then it is definitely the time to change. I tried many times, but the fact I didn't succeed means that I wasn't serious about it.

If the change doesn't occur in a very long period of time despite many efforts is either because you are doing something wrong or not enough. Change strategy after you did your best to follow one without a break. Adapt and keep working on yourself. Don't give up. It's not the strategy that is useless, you are doing it wrong.

We have seen people who are not smart being extremely prosperous.

"I don't have the looks." – How many actors, models who don't look that good, quite the contrary, are incredibly successful? Why do you think is that? Because they were born to get in life what they wanted? We were all born to get in life what we want, but we are weak and don't do the work. These people did everything in their powers to be in movies. To play the role of their lives. They didn't stop at anything. They woke up at 4 am, went to the gym, then knocked on every door they found. When they were turned down, they knocked again, and again, and again until someone opened and let them in. Most people give up at the first try, "It was so humiliating. They didn't even look at me. I can't go through this again."

If you think that after a few attempts, of course you give up. I felt that when I gave up. I cried like a baby in the corner of a room and swore I will never embarrass myself in front of anyone again. But when at forty I realised there was no other way. So I started doing what those who made it do. With the mentality I had, the sensitivity, the sense of guilt, was impossible to get anywhere. I had to make a paradigm shift first. And it wasn't easy. If for 40 years you are a victim, taking life in your own hands triggers a war inside you. Mind, body, and soul in conflict for 24 hours a day is utterly exhausting. That's why most of us don't stick with the decision to change. Surviving is easy, living is an endless tussle.

Everybody wants to have an easy life. We would love to sit all day long, watching TV or walking around, have someone to serve us while we swim in luxury. Some of you will contest this with vehemence, "I don't want to walk around, I want to have a job I love, money to travel, a family to love me. I want to have a purpose."

Well, if you really want that, you go and make it happen. Humans flew to the moon. That was impossible, changing is not that risky and definitely not that expensive. If I can do it, everyone can do it. After 2 years of holding on to my decision to change my thoughts in order to transform my life, I am still having troubles breathing. Like right now. And the reason for this is that I am doing something my body doesn't like to do, insisting on believing I can live one day on my own terms. Everything in my body screams, 'Give up, you fool. You have a good job that allows you to pay the bills. What else do you want? Many would love to be in your position. Stay back and relax. That's what most people do.

You don't have to fight against yourself. You have a destiny that it will fulfil no matter what;   Why do you make everything so complicated?

***

To read more go to https://goo.gl/4R9oVm

It's a great self-growth tool. Discipline, Determination, Grit.

About the Author

Cristina G. was born in Romania during one of the most oppressive communist regimes that ever existed.

She is the tenth child – the seventh daughter – of a family of twelve.

On the 25th of December of 1989, the leaders of her country were shot dead. Christmas, a joyful celebration, has gained a bloody façade for Romanians with a sensitive soul.

Aged eight she fell in love with reading and realised that only books made her feel free.

In 2000 Cristina G. immigrated to Italy where she learnt that people cursed by geography are considered of inferior birth. Ten years later, deprived of dignity and covered in deep wounds, she went back to her country only to find out that freedom without opportunities is just another kind of prison.

Encouraged by her brother, Sebastian, Cristina G. dedicated many years to blogging. Now she is the owner of two very popular blogs in Romanian and one in English.

In 2014, helped by a British friend, Cristina G. moved to the UK where her expectations were not great. Here, against all odds and despite the Brexit Referendum, Cristina G. has finally managed to fulfil a dream she never dared to dream before: becoming a registered author.

Cristina G. invests absolutely everything into this dream: time, money, energy, body and soul.

All her books narrate stories of love and survival. Many are either entirely real or based on reality.

Discrimination, immigration, abuse, self-growth are her main topics.

With a unique, eclectic style that focuses on human behaviour, in two years Cristina G. has written and self-published a couple of memoirs, a collection of short stories, a self-help publication, and three novels.

The reviews are outstanding due to her terrific determination, honesty, and passion.

With an astonishing background, outstanding determination, and remarkable passion, Cristina G. is a perfect candidate to greatness.

Her motto is, "Breathe, Love, Write and Believe."

Cristina G. writes so she could build a bathroom with running water for her beloved octogenarian parents.

If you liked this book, why not review it on Amazon or Goodreads?

Also by Cristina G.

- Oranges at Christmas in a Communist Country – A Memoir – Already in this book
- Ten Years in Italy, Three Weeks a Human – A Memoir – Already in this book
- It's Never Game Over – A Self Help Publication
- God is Weary – Collection of Short and not so Short Tragic and Witty Stories
- iLive – Family can Kill You
- Half my Age Plus Seven – A Sinful Confession
- Half my Age Plus Seven – Too Good to be True?